Porcupine Mountains Wilderness State Park

A Backcountry Guide for Hikers, Backpackers, Campers and Winter Visitors

3rd Edition

D1550947

Porcupine Mountains Wilderness State Park

A Backcountry Guide for Hikers, Backpackers, Campers and Winter Visitors

3rd Edition

by Jim DuFresne

Holt, Michigan

Porcupine Mountains Wilderness State Park, 3rd Edition
©2009 Jim DuFresne

Published by Thunder Bay Press
Holt, Michigan

First Edition 1993
Second Edition 1999
Third Edition 2009

13 12 11 10 09   5 4 3 2 1

ISBN: 978-1-933272-16-0

Photos by Jim DuFresne except where credited
Front cover photo by Steve Brimm, www.brimmages.com
Back cover bear photo by David Kenyon, Michigan DNR
Book and cover design by Julie Taylor

Printed in the United States of America
by McNaughton & Gunn, Inc.

CONTENTS

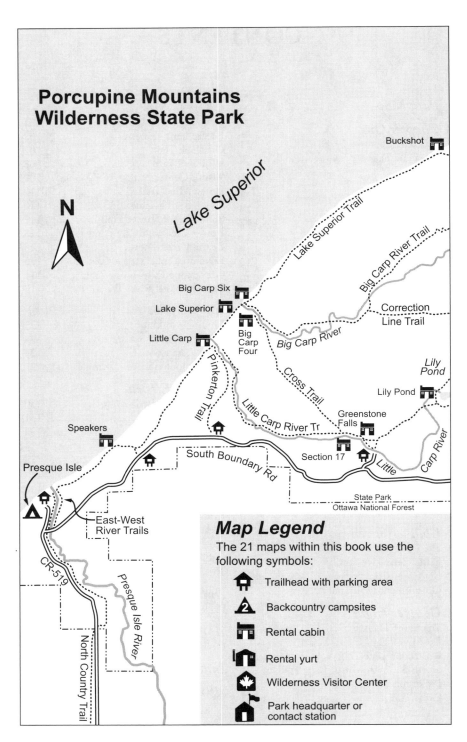

Porcupine Mountains Wilderness State Park

N

Lake Superior

Buckshot

Lake Superior Trail

Big Carp River Trail

Big Carp Six

Lake Superior

Correction Line Trail

Little Carp

Big Carp Four

Big Carp River

Pinkerton Trail

Cross Trail

Lily Pond

Lily Pond

Little Carp River Tr

Greenstone Falls

Speakers

Little Carp River Tr

Section 17

Little Carp River

Presque Isle

South Boundary Rd

State Park
Ottawa National Forest

East-West River Trails

CR-519

Presque Isle River

North Country Trail

Map Legend

The 21 maps within this book use the following symbols:

Trailhead with parking area

2 Backcountry campsites

Rental cabin

Rental yurt

Wilderness Visitor Center

Park headquarter or contact station

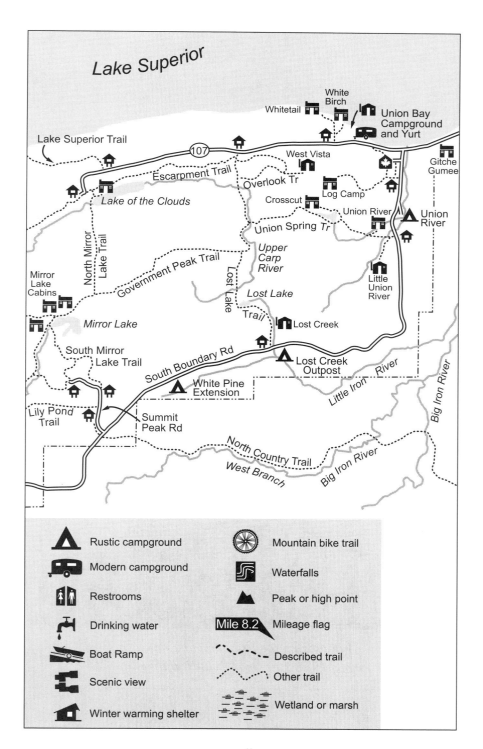

Legend:

- Rustic campground
- Modern campground
- Restrooms
- Drinking water
- Boat Ramp
- Scenic view
- Winter warming shelter
- Mountain bike trail
- Waterfalls
- Peak or high point
- Mile 8.2 Mileage flag
- Described trail
- Other trail
- Wetland or marsh

Views from the Escarpment Trail,
one of Michigan's most beautiful hikes.

Chapter One
A PLACE CALLED THE PORKIES

Something moved. In the shadowy light of a full moon, my task of filling the water bottles was interrupted when in the corner of my eye I saw movement on the other side of Little Carp River. Or I thought I did.

I studied the black trunks of the hardwoods and pines, the silhouettes of bushes and stumps, but on this October evening all was quiet and still in the heart of the Porcupine Mountains. I was on the verge of returning to my chore when a shadow moved again—three steps this way, one step that way. It stopped; I stood up. It turned towards me; I peered into the darkness at it. And suddenly we were both conscious of each other.

Man meets bear in a place called the Porkies.

We both might have bolted into the woods, but 20 yards of rushing water gave us a sense of security so we took the opportunity to study each other a little bit longer. The few black bears I had encountered in Michigan looked little more than a large dog. This one had some bulk to it... a 250-pound bear? Maybe a 300-pounder? When it turned sideways, the shadow the moonlight cast of my backwoods companion was even more impressive.

"Whoa!" I said softly under my breath.

It inched closer to the riverbank, nuzzled this with its nose, pawed that with its claws, and then stopped again to look at me. Only 30 yards separated us and now the bear appeared to be squinting at me.

"Gotta go," I said in a booming voice so there was no question in its mind as to what I was. I retreated up the bank in three steps or less, and after reaching the top I turned to the river again.

The bear was gone. It vanished into the shadows from which it emerged without leaving a trace of its movement.

I sat down on a stump and wondered what else was out there when the spirit of this wilderness descended upon me, like it always does at such moments. It's not picturesque Lake of the Clouds or the views from Summit Peak, as nice as they are, that make some of us return year after year to Porcupine Mountains Wilderness State Park. It's the feeling of being out there in a land where man is at best a visitor passing through. It's the idea that this rugged corner of the Upper Peninsula has been explored and mapped and even laced with foot trails and backcountry cabins, but never tamed. Like a fortress against development and that oxymoron we call "progress," the Porkies have always been this place where you retreated to rediscover yourself and the natural world around you.

It's a timeless quality first experienced by the Indians and then acknowledged by those early miners. Today it's a priceless quality that attracts thousands of visitors who merely want to wander down a path or pause in wonder along the rocky shoreline of Lake Superior. The billboards, the golden arches, the motorized pace of our society is somewhere else.

Out here it's towering pines 300 years old and spectacular waterfalls. It's sweeping views from rocky knobs reached by the slow and thoughtful pace of foot travel that keeps everything in proper perspective.

If only for a few days, leave your vehicle, slow down, and look around. There's a bear on the other side of the river.

A Place Called The Porkies

The Porcupine Mountains, like Isle Royale, the Keweenaw Peninsula, and much of the Lake Superior basin was born during the Precambrian era, some 1.2 billion years ago when lava seeped up through the cracks of the earth and formed basalt, the bedrock of the area. After each lava flow, wind and rain carried sand, gravel and other sediments, producing layers of soft rock between the hard slabs of basalt.

Eventually the center began to subside and this warp, called the Lake Superior Syncline, created the basin of the Great Lake while the raised and titled layers of rock became its borders. Over thousands of years the bands of basalt have withstood forces of nature to remain as ridges while the softer layers of rock eroded away to form the valleys and inland lakes between them.

Nowhere is this more evident than the escarpment along Lake

Superior, known by geologists at the Outer or Great Conglomerate. The domal warp resulted in a ridge that rises 900 feet above Lake Superior and then gives way to a 400-foot escarpment leading to the valley that contains Lake of the Clouds and Carp Creek. This pattern is repeated in a more subdued form to give the park its "mountainous" topography.

Technically the Porkies are not mountains. A geologist defines such topography as a spot 2,000 feet or higher. The highest point in the state park is Summit Peak, which at 1,958 feet is one of the highest "mountains" between the Black Hills of South Dakota and New York's Adirondacks but still 42 feet short of fulfilling a geologist's definition. True mountain or not, backpackers today still take notice of the sharp climbs to the top of the ridges and so did the Native Americans. The eroded edges of the park's escarpment and the gentle northern slope to Lake Superior were described by the first Indians as "crouched porcupines," hence the name Porcupine Mountains.

On top of the Summit Peak observation tower,
looking at the interior of the state park.

Indians began wandering into the area as early as 1750 B.C. They struggled over the ridges and escarpments during the summer in an effort to mine copper. Using fire and water, they fractured boulders, pounded out the metal, and shaped it into tools, ornaments, and projectile points. Some archaeologists have estimated that the ancient miners extracted more than 500 million pounds of copper from an area that included the Porkies, Isle Royale, and the Keweenaw Peninsula and then traded it throughout Eastern North America.

It was not copper that brought the first Europeans into the area, but, rather, furs. The great North American fur trade that spread across the Great Lakes in the late 1700s was responsible for the first white settlements in the Porkies in the form of trading posts at the outlets of the Iron and Presque Isle Rivers. The bands of Ojibway Indians soon forgot their clay pots and copper tools for the guns, iron kettles, and axes they could obtain with beaver pelts and other furs.

By 1837 the fur trade was winding down when Michigan became a state. That year its young governor, Stevens T. Mason, appointed Douglas Houghton as State Geologist and appropriated funds for a geological survey to map the Upper Peninsula's unknown wealth of natural resources.

Houghton and his team accomplished a great deal during their journey. They collected plant and mineral specimens, mapped swamps, rivers, and lakes, reported on timber and the quality of soil. However it was his geological survey that drew the most attention. It was published in 1841 and told of the copper deposits in the Western Upper Peninsula. One man's report, yet it was all that was needed to create the first great mining rush in American history as men swarmed into copper country in search of fortunes they were sure were hidden in the rocks.

The first mining effort in the Porkies was the Union Mine that was started in 1845 as the Isle Royale and Lake Superior Mine near the Union River. William W. Spalding was in charge of the operation, and the remains of the first shaft can still be seen today along the Union Mine Trail near interpretive post number one. Spalding eventually found a vein of copper, but little profit was ever realized by the early investors.

In 1864 the company was sold to a Detroit businessman. Four more shafts were sunk, one up to 400 feet deep, and a steam-powered stamping mill used for crushing ore was brought in. Eventually the entire operation was given up due to exorbitant production and shipping costs versus the low grade of ore.

This was the story for the 45 mines started in the Porcupine Mountains. The copper veins rarely could turn a profit for the investors, who on the average spent five times more extracting the metal than it was worth on the open market. While solid copper masses of several hundred tons were found in mines east of Ontonagon, including a pure 3,708-pound nugget known as the Ontonagon Boulder that today rests in the Smithsonian Institute, the Porkies copper existed in small particles and flakes within the rock. Without the rich veins of copper, the only time mines, like the Union, LaFayette, Halliwell, and Cuyahoga, turned a profit was when the Civil War demand for the metal drove the prices high enough to overcome the production costs.

The last mine in the area was the Nonesuch, which opened in 1867. Located south of the Union Mine, the Nonesuch was operated off and on until 1910. At its peak the operation boasted a rail tram to its Union Bay docks, twelve log homes, an agent's residence, general store, post office, a stagecoach, even a uniformed baseball team. It also swallowed several large fortunes while producing only 180 tons of refined copper during its 43-year existence. Today, remains of of the mine can still be viewed by continuing on a dirt road where South Boundary Road curves west, 4.3 miles south of M-107.

There were some attempts to mine silver, which proved no more profitable than copper. Then in the early 1900s, as the mining era was ending, the logging began. From Lone Rock east to Cuyahoga Gap, lumberjacks concentrated on the shoreline pines but passed up the rugged interior of the Porkies for more accessible tracts elsewhere.

The only other major logging in the present park occurred following a devastating natural disaster. On the morning of June 30, 1953, tornado-force winds raged across Lake Superior and finally touched land near the mouth of the Big Carp River. The gale proceeded to cut a two-mile-wide path through the forest in which trunks two-feet in diameter were twisted and snapped like match sticks. Faced with 1,200 acres of fallen trees that represented more than 10 million board feet, the park staff allowed loggers to enter the park and salvage the wood.

The rest of the Porkies' interior remained unmolested by miners, loggers and other entrepreneurs. By the 1930s the Porcupine Mountains were a rare remnant of the virgin forest which once had stretched from the Mississippi River to the Atlantic Ocean and was soon being referred to as a "forest museum." Eventually the federal government designated the Porkies as a potential site for the next national park, but the plans were abandoned by the financially strapped Congress at the start of World War II. When the war demand for lumber renewed the loggers' interest for the interior timber, concerned citizens and the state did what the federal government could not.

Global conflict or not, this distant corner of Michigan, the largest stand of virgin maple and hemlock between the Rockies and the Adirondacks, was too precious to be stripped just for its trees. A push for the Porkies preservation resulted in it becoming a state park in 1945, and in 1946, its first year as an operational unit, Porcupine Mountains State Park drew 70,000 visitors.

State park status was not enough, however, to keep the mining and logging interests at bay. Over the years not only were developers eyeing the resources of the Porkies, but politicians proposed such schemes that ranged from building a road along Lake Superior to a push for a dog racing track in the park. The management and protection of the Porkies finally peaked in heated controversy that ended when the state passed the Wilderness and Natural Areas Act in 1972, and the park officially became known as Porcupine Mountains Wilderness State Park.

"It was almost a national park and it really is a national park quality resource," said one park manager. "Few state parks have the resource base that the Porkies have."

Or the dimensions. Although the majority of the 305,000 annual visitors never venture beyond the Lake of the Clouds overlook, a spectacular vista of a lake surrounded by ridges and escarpments, this park is much more than one over-photographed viewing point.

Day hiker takes in Lake of the Clouds from the Escarpment Trail.

Michigan's largest state park is 26 miles long, 10 miles at its widest point, and covers 59,020 acres. Along with peaks that top 1,900 feet, the Porkies contain 25 miles of Lake Superior shoreline, four lakes, entire rivers, trout streams that are choked with spawning salmon in the fall, and 14 waterfalls that are named— dozens more that are not.

There are also more than 90 miles of foot paths that wind through the heart of this wilderness. The longest is the Lake Superior Trail that stretches for 17 miles along the lakeshore. Others say the most scenic trek in the Upper Peninsula is the 4.3-mile hike along the Escarpment Trail which gives way to vistas of sheer cliffs and panoramas of Lake of the Clouds.

Whether it's a half-mile walk to the Greenstone Falls or a four-day trek to the most remote corner of the park, these foot paths are the avenues to the natural treasures the Porkies have protected throughout history.

Michigan's Highest Point

Unlike almost every other state, Michigan's highest point has always been an elusive, hard-to-find place. At first it was thought to be Summit Peak, the 1,958-foot ridge in the Porcupine Mountains Wilderness State Park, crowned today by an observation tower that is easily reached after just a short hike.

But in 1963 Mount Curwood in Baraga County was designated the highest elevation in the state at 1,996 feet. For the next two decades highpointers, whose mission in life is to stand on the highest point in all 50 states, arrived at L'Anse from around the country to follow a maze of logging roads to the remote summit.

Then, much to their disappointment, Michigan's top peak was changed for a third time. In 1982, the Department of Interior conducted a survey and concluded Mount Curwood is really only 1,978.24 feet in elevation and the second highest spot in the state. Michigan's loftiest peak is nearby Mount Arvon, which at 1,979.238 feet above sea level is less than a foot higher than Curwood.

A local Boy Scout troop became the first group to climb Mount Arvon (GPS: North 45° 45.330', West 88° 9.325') after it's new designation and built a yellow witness box at the top. Inside is a log book for people to leave their name, the date they reached the top and the number of other high points they have visited.

In 1999, the route to Mount Arvon was improved and signposted while on the peak itself a "Congratulations! You have reached Michigan's Highest Point" sign was installed. There is also a USGS brass marker verifying the elevation. What you won't find at the top is much of a view.

In the summer and fall, the view is obscured by foliage. In late November, after the leaves have fallen but before the snows arrive, you can wander to north side of the roundish peak and through the trees gaze out on Lake Superior, Huron Bay, and Point Abbaye which separates the two.

For a map and a precise set of directions to Mt. Arvon, contact the Baraga County Tourist and Recreation Association:

800-743-4908, 906-524-7444
www.baragacountytourism.org

Flora and Fauna

Despite the best efforts of miners and loggers, the rugged interior of the Porcupine Mountains kept most of man's activity confined to its edges and outer regions. The result is that today the Porkies support the largest stand of old growth hardwood and hemlock forest between the Adirondacks and the Rocky Mountains.

Almost 60 percent of the state park, or 35,000 acres, remains virgin timber with the forest being dominated by hemlock and northern hardwoods such as sugar maple, basswood, and yellow birch. Miners eagerly sought out the yellow birch and maple for its dense wood which was used in the supporting timbers of their mines and, more importantly, the production of charcoal to fuel the steam engines in the stamp mills.

On north facing slopes hemlock becomes the dominate species and often is found in almost pure stands while swamps and low-lying areas are forested by tamarack and white cedar. Miners also had an eye for the cedar as its resistance to rot when in contact with the soil made it their first choice for support beams in the shafts.

In the flood plains of the Carp Rivers and other streams, you encounter white spruce and black ash while much of the area between M-107 and Lake Superior is made up of aspen and paper birch. This is the result of the heavy shoreline logging that took place in the early 1900s and the slash fires that followed, reducing the land to bare rock.

A variety of wild berries thrives in the park including bearberry and blueberry, best encountered along the crests and cliffs of the front ranges. On the forest floor there is often an abundance of thimbleberries, a tart edible fruit which is a favorite with local jam makers. The waist-high bush has a large maple-like leaf, a white blossom, and berries that ripen from July to mid-August.

Wildlife in the park ranges from deer, fish, river otters, beavers, porcupines, and red squirrels to a variety of birds including goshawks, peregrine falcons, barred owl, and bald eagles. In the fall it is possible to stand on the bridge near the mouth of the Big Carp River and watch Chinook salmon gather in the pools for a spawning run upstream.

The park also supports coyotes, bobcats, pine martens, and a growing number of wolves. Once hunted into extinction in Michigan, wolves returned by migrating from northern Minnesota, and in 1991 there were seventeen animals in the Upper Peninsula. Today it is estimated there are more than 500 while in 2005 two wolves were spotted in the Lower Peninsula's Emmet County.

Biologists believe two packs, one with up to a dozen members and the other with four to five wolves, roam the general area in and around the Porcupine Mountains. Encounters with a wolf, however, is highly unlikely as the animal tends to be shy and avoids human encounters at all costs.

After being re-introduced to the Upper Peninsula in the mid-1980s, three or four moose also live in the park and occasionally are seen by visitors feeding at Lake of the Clouds. The animal that commands the most attention here, however, is the black bear. The rugged and wooded terrain of the Porkies is good habitat for bruins, and biologists estimate that the area supports a bear for every 3 to 4 square miles for roughly a total population that fluctuates between 25 and 40.

Among the wildlife hikers might encounter are whitetail deer,
maybe even a trophy buck if they are lucky.
(Michigan DNR photo by David Kenyon)

*Biologists estimate that two or three moose live
in Porcupine Mountains Wilderness State Park.*

A two to three-year-old bear averages 150 pounds and looks like a large, rounded dog when on all fours, but large males have been known to weigh in at 300 to 400 pounds. While bears are carnivorous, they feed on roots, berries, whatever they find in the woods, and occasionally a deer fawn. They may appear to be slow, but bears can easily outrun a person while a 200-pound bruin can crawl through an opening that would be a squeeze for even a child.

Bears begin denning in early October and are in a hibernation-like sleep for the winter by mid-November, not emerging from their caves until March or April. Sows breed every other year with an average litter ranging from one to two cubs although biologists have recorded litters as large as five. Cubs weigh around a half pound at birth and stay with the mother through the following winter.

Most bear sightings in the Porkies occur during the spring when two-year-olds are forced away from their mother for the first time. No matter when you are at the state park it's important to practice good bear precautions, especially if you are traveling or camping in the backcountry (see chapter 2). It's equally important to realize that a bear has never seriously injured a visitor in the Porkies and that a small percentage of backpackers even see them during the summer. What you will often spot are their tracks. A bear print looks more like a human foot than a dog track, but it has a more rounded pad and claws that can usually be clearly seen off the toes. A track four inches or wider is a sign of a good size bear.

While a few bruins will raid the suspended food sacks of backpackers every summer, biologists will quickly point out that most have a healthy respect for people and simply turn and run when encountered. They seen to understand there is little to gain by exposing themselves.

A backpacker pauses at Presque Isle River at the beginning of her trek along the Lake Superior Trail.

Chapter Two
ENJOYING THE PORKIES

There is a group of us who get together to do nothing but hike and eat. We're backpacking gourmets; we may sleep on the ground but we eat like kings. We sharpen our appetite with long treks into the woods and then enjoy scrumptious meals with a view from our plate that few restaurants in Michigan can match.

One summer, with packs bulging with shallots, sour cream, and wine in a box (minus the box), we entered Porcupine Mountains Wilderness State Park for four days of gastronomic adventures. The rules of the outing were simple. Each of us was in charge of an entire meal, from pre-trip planning and preparation to serving it and washing the pots. All ingredients had to be obtained from the average supermarket. That's especially important, for if I ate four or five days of freeze-dried "meal-in-a-pouch" dinners I'd have enough gas to drive home.

I had dinner on the third day and the culinary competition was tough. We had already eaten our way through Chicken Cacciatore, Eggs Benedict, freshly baked croissants (somebody packed in an Outback Oven for baking) and No-Bake Drop Cookies for dessert one night (clever, clever, we all remarked).

With a determination to finally capture the coveted trophy (a leftover bag of gorp), I went to work in the middle of the wilderness when we stopped for a night at the mouth of the Big Carp River. My appetizers were a selection of smoked trout and sharp cheddar cheeses served with an English hardsauce. The next course was cream of asparagus soup (dried soup mix from International Bazaar), followed by a marinated cabbage salad that was marinating as we hiked in, and the main entree of Fettuccine with Sausage Ragout Sauce.

"How did you pack in the sweet Italian sausage?" asked one of my critics.

"It's dried sausage that I reconstituted."

"Why isn't the fettuccine all broken from three days at the

bottom of your pack?" asked another.

"It's fresh pasta."

But the coup de grâce came at the end. For dessert I walked down to Lake Superior and from the frigid waters pulled out a tightly sealed pot that contained individual cheese cakes (the key was the miniature Ready Crusts by Keebler). I topped off the well-chilled dessert with a fruit sauce made from dried cherries and served them with what I call "Campfire Capuccino", a hot drink that contains, among other ingredients, a Hershey chocolate bar, instant coffee, Grand Marnier, and a layer of melted marshmallow at the top instead of steamed milk.

They gave me a standing ovation and the bag of half eaten gorp. Then on the shores of Lake Superior, facing one of the most beautiful panoramas in Michigan, we indulged in dessert and after dinner drinks until the setting sun had turned the Great Lake blazing orange. And some people think wilderness treks and good cuisine are incompatible!

Visiting The Park

Porcupine Mountains Wilderness State Park draws more than 305,000 visitors annually, and from May through October when the vast majority arrive, they can easily be divided into three categories. The most common is a day visitor, who arrives to take in the panorama from the Lake of the Clouds Escarpment, view the exhibits at the visitor's center and possibly have a picnic along the shores of Lake Superior. Then they're off to other attractions in the U.P., often spending less than two hours in the park.

Then there are the campers, who stay for a night or more in one of the five campgrounds on the edge of the park. Their journeys into the interior of the Porkies are strictly day hikes where they can travel without the burden of having to carry heavy loads in a backpack and by nightfall are back in the comfort of a trailer or a spacious tent at their site.

Finally, there are the backcountry users, visitors who leave their cars at the trailheads. They take to the paths in order to spend every minute of their stay deep in the mountains, either by booking a trailside cabin in advance or carrying in a tent.

To get the most out of any trip to this park, it's best to know what is available and plan accordingly, especially if reservations are required. Cabins, yurts, and campgrounds are covered in chapter 3, trails in chapters 6 through 10, and the winter facilities and ski trails in chapter 11, but here are the day-use areas and other facilities:

Headquarters:

The park headquarters (906-885-5275) is across from the Wilderness Visitor Center off South Boundary Road. The office is open year round, Monday through Friday from 8 a.m. to 4:30 p.m. (EST) and can provide maps, handle cabin and campground reservations, and provide information about all the park's facilities and activities.

Wilderness Visitor Center:

The first stop for any person just arriving at the park, day visitor or backcountry user, should be the park's impressive Wilderness Visitor Center, located a half mile south of M-107 on South Boundary Road. Inside there are exhibits explaining everything about the park from its creation and history of the miners to its flora and wildlife, including a display devoted to black bears. There is also a 100-seat auditorium where a multi-image slide program about the park is shown throughout the day. Perhaps the most interesting item, at least to anybody who plans to hike the trails, is the three-dimensional relief map that gives one a good idea just how rugged the Porkies really are.

The visitor center also serves as the main registration station. Backpackers planning to overnight in the park's backcountry can obtain wilderness camping permits here and the latest information on trail conditions and black bear sightings or purchase maps and books. The staff also can assist visitors with information on campgrounds, trailside cabins, and other facilities. The center is open daily from 10 a.m. to 6 p.m. (EST), from late May through mid-October.

Picnic Areas:

There is a picnic area on each side of the park adjacent to the two major campgrounds. On the east side, near the Union Bay

Campground, picnic tables are situated along the Lake Superior shoreline along M-107. Across the road a short trail leads to the Visitor Center. On the west side the picnic area is passed just before entering the Presque Isle Campground and includes a shelter as well as tables, vault toilets, and pedestal grills. A meal here is enhanced even more with a short stroll down the boardwalk to the picturesque mouth of the Presque Isle River.

Lake of the Clouds Scenic Area:

At the end of M-107, it's a short walk to perhaps Michigan's most famous panorama. The overlook is set on the side of the escarpment, a vertical cliff basically, and from the high point of 1,375 feet it is possible to see the Porkies' rugged interior and the picturesque Lake of the Clouds set among the forested ridges. Displays near the parking area explain the geology of the escarpment while three trails, Big Carp River, Escarpment and North Mirror Lake, depart from here. There are picnic tables and toilets located here but no source of water.

Summit Peak Scenic Area:

The other spectacular viewing point in the park is the tower on Summit Peak, the highest point in the Porkies at 1,958 feet. A trip to the observation deck begins with a drive up the winding Summit Peak Road through towering timber. Once on top you follow a path a half mile to the 40-foot high tower. The view spans the interior of the Porkies while on a clear day it's possible to see Copper Peak along the Black River and even Apostle Islands off Wisconsin. Facilities include tables and a toilet building but no source of water.

Presque Isle Scenic Area:

At the west end of the park this scenic area includes a half mile of boardwalks and viewing platforms that put visitors right on top of swirling rapids and the most impressive waterfalls in the park. The Presque Isle River is often regarded as Michigan's wildest, especially the final mile just before it empties into Lake Superior. Along with the boardwalk and the East and West River Trails (see chapter 9), the area includes a picnic area, restrooms, an overnight backpacker's parking lot, and a semi-modern campground.

Information

For information in advance you can contact the park headquarters (906-885-5275; Porcupine Mountains Wilderness State Park, 412 South Boundary Rd., Ontonagon, MI 49953). You can also access information and brochures on the park web site (*www.michigan.gov/porkies*).

Founded in 1998 to help promote and support the state park is the Friends of the Porkies (906-884-4274; www.porkies.org; P.O. Box 221, Ontonagon, MI 49953). You can contact them in regard to a variety of events they sponsor in the park including the Porcupine Mountains Music Festival staged in August, a folk music school, and an artist-in-residence program, where photographers, writers, and artists are provided with the use of a cabin within the park.

The group also funds the Porcupine Mountains Visitor, a publication that is dedicated to visiting the park and is updated annually. You can request one in advance from the park headquarters or download it online from the Michigan DNR site (*www.michigan.gov/dnr*) by clicking on "Recreation, Camping & Boating," then "Visitor Centers, Museums & Historic Sites" and finally "Wilderness Visitor Center."

Permits & Fees

Whether you plan to be in the park for an hour or a week, you need to have either a daily vehicle permit or an annual state park pass. These can be purchased at various contact stations in the park, the Visitor Center, or the park headquarters. A state park pass allows you unlimited entry to any unit in the Michigan State Park system for the year.

All overnight hikers must also register before embarking on their trek, and each party must obtain a rustic camping permit if they are not staying in a cabin. There is a per night fee for the permits which can be obtained at the Wilderness Visitor Center, the park headquarters, or the contact stations at Presque Isle or Union Bay campgrounds. After business hours, you may also self-register at trailhead kiosks located at Presque Isle, Lake of the Clouds Scenic Area, Summit Peak Scenic Area, and the park headquarters.

Day Hiking

No permit is needed to spend a day hiking in the backcountry, but you must still purchase a vehicle entry permit or an annual state park pass. Trailheads are marked on the park map and posted along M-107, South Boundary Road, and at the Presque Isle day-use area. Small parking lots are near most of the trailheads although at times in mid-summer they could easily be filled with vehicles.

Even if you are only day hiking, don't under estimate the park's ruggedness. Most day hikers need 40 minutes to an hour to cover a mile of trail, depending on their physical condition. The trails are well marked and, for the most part, easy to follow, but still pack along a map, drinking water, compass, and a small flashlight in case you lag behind after the sun sets. Most importantly, bring a parka or jacket for protection against a sudden turn in the weather. The last thing you want is to get caught in the middle of the Porkies in shorts and a t-shirt when a storm blows in unexpectedly.

A backpacker fords the Big Carp River.

Rivers Without Bridges

More so in the Porkies than anywhere else in Michigan, backpackers should know how to ford a river correctly. The majority of the streams in the park do not have a bridge across them although this is rarely a problem. The best place to cross is usually easy to identify by the string of ideally-positioned boulders across it. Many hikers will then switch from their boots to a pair of sport sandals or running shoes before tiptoeing across the rocks or splashing through the stream. Others simply accept wet boots for the rest of the day and forge ahead. Never cross a river barefoot.

Immediately after a heavy rainfall is a different story. You might have to search for a better spot upstream. If the water is deeper than your thighs, turn back and look for another place to cross. If the stream is especially swift, turn back when it reaches your knees.

And sometimes you might not be able to ford at all. In June of 1983 a storm dumped 13 inches of rain on the Porkies resulting in all the park's rivers becoming dangerously swollen. The worst flooding, however, occurred along the Little Carp River below Lily Pond. The water rose to depths of 30 feet, stranding several backpacking parties, wiping out bridges, and causing mud slides on bluffs and hills bordering the Little Carp.

Backcountry Camping

Unless you have reserved a wilderness cabin or yurt in advance (See chapter 3), once in the backcountry you will be pitching a tent. Scattered throughout the park are 63 backcountry campsites that include metal fire rings, open-air vault toilets, and in many cases bear poles. There are twenty sites along the Lake Superior Trail with seven more on the shores of Mirror Lake, five on Lake of the Clouds, and ten stretched along the Little Carp River Trail. Each site accommodates a hiking party with twelve people being the maximum number allowed to stay at one. The per night costs depends on the number of people in your party. The sites are also used on a first-come, first serve basis and, because of their close proximity to these major features of the park, are the choice of many looking for a place to pitch their tents. In the busy months of July or August, be prepared to move on or camp off trail in case the sites are already occupied. On the maps, the location and number of sites are denoted with this symbol: ▲.

Finally, off-trail camping is permitted throughout the park, except within a quarter mile of any cabin, scenic area such as an inland lake or waterfall, or road. Nor do you want to actually pitch a tent on the side of the trail. Keep your camps discreet and unobtrusive, and be sure when you depart that the area looks as if you were never there to begin with.

Backcountry Needs

The Porkies are rugged. If you're planning to travel or overnight in the backcountry prepare for them as you would any wilderness. Arrive with the gear you will need to be comfortable, but realize that this is one place where you do not want to be hauling around a 50 or 60-pound pack.

Hiking Boots:

Flimsy tennis shoes or running shoes will not do for hiking in the Porkies. There are ridges to climb, roots to stumble over, and rocks to traverse. For these kind of conditions you need a pair of good, well-designed hiking boots. The ultralight nylon and leather boots that dominate the market today provide excellent foot protection for any trek in the park. Just make sure you toss an extra pair of wool socks into your pack along with a first aid kit for feet (moleskin, bandages, blister cream).

Stove:

Campfires in the park are limited to designated fire rings, making a lightweight backpacking stove, such as the Whisperlite from MSR, a necessity. Whether you plan to rent a cabin or pitch a tent, do all your cooking on a small stove. It will make meal preparation a lot easier and faster. You will soon discover down wood is a scarce item in many popular backcountry areas. The desire for nightly campfires literally strips the surrounding woods of fallen timber before the summer is over.

Clothes:

If you are arriving during the summer, come prepared for cool, wet weather. Then when the sun breaks out and the temperatures hit 80 degrees, you won't mind lugging around the extra clothes.

Even in the middle of the summer, the nights can be cool, and the wind off Lake Superior can rip right through you. If you're planning a backpacking adventure or extensive day hiking, make sure you pack along rain gear, preferably both parka and pants. On overnight treks, you should also have an insulating layer for those all-day rainstorms or a sudden drop in the temperature. For that layer, most hikers use a jersey of fleece fabric such as Polartec rather than a wool sweater. Like wool, the pile will keep you warm when wet, but it dries much faster. Avoid taking any cotton, as it will not insulate when wet and takes forever to dry.

For trips to the park in spring and fall, you need even more protection against wet and cold weather, including wool hat, mittens and even lightweight polypropylene underwear.

Tent:

A tent in the backcountry serves two purposes: keeping you dry inside and keeping the bugs outside. Make sure your unit has a rain-fly and bug-proof netting. Pack along a quality sleeping pad, such as a Thermarest, to place under your sleeping bag, and you shouldn't have any problem getting a good sleep at night… not after all the ridges you climbed that day.

Water:

All water taken from the rivers and lakes, even Lake Superior, should either be boiled for a minute or run through a 0.5 micron filter system designed to remove the cyst, *Giardia lamblia*. That means packing a reliable filter system or enough gas to boil water every day. Drinking water is available at Union Bay or Presque Isle campgrounds.

Other Equipment:

Bugs are a fact of life in any wilderness area. Bring an insect repellent, especially in June and July, and still pray for a steady wind off Lake Superior. Every hiking party should have a map and compass and the knowledge to use them correctly. The park is covered by three USGS topographical sections (scale 1:62,500); Thomaston, White Pine, and Carp River. The Visitor Center also sells a map that covers the elevation and trails of the entire park that is much more updated but lacks the detail of USGS topos.

Jim DuFresne's Better Trail Mix Recipe

3 Large Bags of M&Ms
1 Ziplock plastic bag

Open bags of M&Ms and pour into the plastic bag. Mix well. Hey, why not? In the world of backpackers I am known as an M&M picker. I pick out the candy first and eat the nuts and raisins only when there is nothing left. I might as well make trail mix that's nothing but M&Ms. If this puts you too much on a guilt trip then throw in a handful of those whole wheat crunches so you can call it "healthy" while still consuming entire bags of it in the backcountry.

When To Go

The park is open year-round, and the frost-free period is from June to September. Not surprisingly, that is also when most visitors arrive in the park, especially from late June through mid-August.

Do insects horrify you? Keep in mind that the U.P. has a black fly season that occurs for a week or two from mid-May through mid-June and many feel that this insect is by far the most irritant one in the backcountry. Stable flies, which appear like biting houseflies, can also be particularly annoying and generally peak sometime from the third week of June to Fourth of July. Beyond those flies you are left to deal with mosquitoes, deer flies, an occasional swarm of no-see-ums, gnats, and other assorted species. By mid-August the number of insects begins to taper down and by early September they are rarely noticed.

In my opinion, the ideal time to visit the park is in September. Fall colors peak around the third week of the month and are spectacular at this park. There is no worry about bugs, and the summer rush of hikers has long since left the campgrounds and backcountry. If you are looking for what many refer to as a "wilderness experience" (four days without a Big Mac), September through mid-October is the best time to look for it in the Porkies.

Deer hunters move in on November 15 for the 16-day firearm hunt, and the winter season generally begins by mid-December though a good snowfall in November is not uncommon. Both downhill and Nordic skiing traditionally last through the month of March.

Porcupine Mountains has a healthy population of black bears. Biologists estimate 25 to 40 live in and around the park. (Michigan DNR photo by David Kenyon)

Bears

Bears are encountered in the park though not nearly as often as most visitors expect. The reality is that the vast majority of hikers and backpackers never see a bruin during their stay in the Porkies. Because of their keen sense of smell, most bears would only visit a camp if attracted by the odor of food or some other attractive scent.

Thus, a little common sense will prevent any problem with bears, and that begins with never feeding a bear nor cooking in or around your tent. Do not store food or scented items such as toothpaste in your tent at night. Pack all food in zip-lock style bags, and then "cache" them at night by hanging them in the bear poles that have been erected at many backcountry campsites. The metal poles are two inches in diameter and 15 feet high. A long rod is provided to hang packs and food on hooks at the top of the pole. Since being installed during the mid-1990s, the number of backpacker-bear encounters have been reduced dramatically.

If you are not at a campsite or there is no bear pole, then suspend your food between two trees at least 12 feet off the ground and at least 100 feet away from your camp. Remember, if you can reach the cache, so can most bears. Roadside campers should wash dishes immediately after a meal and then store food in airtight containers in the trunk of the car.

If you do encounter a bear, keep calm and retreat slowly. Never approach a bear cub; the sow is almost always nearby. Don't close in on a bear with a camera in hand.

Encountering a Bear on the Trail

The park staff were able to reduce the vast majority of bear problems in the Porkies with bear poles and, more importantly, education. Teaching visitors, especially those entering the backcountry, not to feed bears was only part of it. They also wanted backpackers to understand the bear itself and what its behavior means.

A bear is studying you if...
- it stands on its hind legs to get a better view
- it waves its nose around smelling the air
- it makes low, non-aggressive grunting sounds

A bear may be getting upset if...
- it clicks its teeth
- it gives a loud blowing sound

A bear is telling you to leave when it...
- blows loudly
- makes short lunges
- hits the ground or nearby objects
- gives a bluff charge that stops short of you

Loving The Porkies To Death

We love the Porkies so much, one ranger told me, we're slowly killing them. And in a way it's true. If we're not conscious of our behavior in the backcountry, the pristine streams and forests that draw us to this remote corner of Michigan will be lost.

The park is fragile, as is all wilderness, and the only way it will survive the thousands that hike and camp here is if we all practice "low impact use" of the area:

• Pack out all trash. You will find trash containers at the trailheads and in campgrounds. Don't leave trash in the cabins or the shelters; the cost of removing it is astronomical. Don't bury refuse. Animals will dig it up and spread it over a large area. Not only pack out your own trash but go a step further. Pick up and carry out the litter someone else thoughtlessly dropped.

• Build campfires only in designated areas and no fires whatsoever during dry weather when there is a high fire danger alert. Burn only down wood and never cut live trees.

• Do not use motorized methods of transportation or wheeled carts on park trails. Use mountain bikes only on trails designated for their use.

• Do not shortcut switchbacks, start new trails, or widen trails when they are wet and muddy. Accept the inevitable: hiking through the mud is part of the backcountry experience and march on.

• Do not wash or throw wastewater into or close to any water source, stream, or lake.

• In the backcountry, bury human waste and tissue paper at least six inches deep.

• Leave the radios and tape recorders at home while visiting the Porkies. The solitude of nature is too rare and valuable to disturb with man-made music.

• And most importantly, when you break camp, leave no trace of yourself.

Beavers are found throughout the state park.

Chapter Three

CAMPGROUNDS, CABINS & YURTS

I'm not a woodsman, nor a person who really gets close to nature. Roughing it to me is staying at the Holiday Inn when I had reservations at the Hilton.

-From the log book in the Big Carp River Six-Bunk Cabin

Spending a night in the Porkies? At one time there was a push to build a luxurious lodge here, primarily to attract more skiers to the downhill slopes. It has yet to be built, but that's not to say the Porkies doesn't have a wide range of lodging possibilities.

Most accommodations in the park are rustic, maybe too rustic for some visitors, but no matter where you unroll your sleeping bag in Michigan it's hard to beat the setting that surrounds you in the Porkies. The two main campgrounds are along Lake Superior, others are situated on small rugged rivers while many of the nineteen cabins can be found near waterfalls, overlooking the Great Lake, even on the shores of Lake of the Clouds.

You can sleep on a mattress in a bunk of a cabin, on the ground in a backcountry campsite, or in your 30-foot recreational vehicle in a campground with warm showers, flush toilets, and an electrical outlet to plug in the microwave oven. Regardless of where you make camp, spending a night or two in the park greatly enhances any visit, especially if you can escape into the backcountry, but plan ahead as to where you want to stay and then make reservations if they are needed. You don't want to be left out in the cold when night falls on the Porkies.

Campgrounds

Scattered along the edge of the park are six campgrounds that accessible from the road:

Union Bay:

This is the largest campground with 99 sites and is the only modern one in the park. Located on the east side, Union Bay is reached from M-107, just beyond South Boundary Road, and consists of a grassy shelf overlooking Lake Superior with little shade. The facilities include showers, modern restrooms, a sanitation station for RVs along with an improved boat launch on Lake Superior. Nearby the Whitetail Path departs along M-107 to the Visitor's Center a mile away.

Union Bay fills occasionally from late July through mid-August. During the rest of the season there are likely to be open sites on almost any day. The restrooms and showers are operated from mid-May through the third week in October.

Presque Isle:

On the west end of the park is Presque Isle Campground, a rustic facility with 50 sites located on a bluff above Lake Superior near the picturesque mouth of its namesake river. The campground can be reached by either following South Boundary Road around the park or from US-2 by heading 17 miles north from Wakefield on County Road 519 to its end.

Presque Isle's large, spaced-out sites are scattered around two loops with a dozen of them on the edge of the bluff overlooking the lake. The rest are in a large grassy area, shaded by a scattering of large maples while the campground itself is surrounded by woods. Facilities include tables, fire rings, vault toilets, and hand pumps for water.

The lack of electricity for RVers and modern restrooms are the reasons, no doubt, why Presque Isle rarely fills to capacity even after it was reduced in size by 33 sites in 2003. Those planning to camp at Presque Isle should keep in mind the nearest gasoline station and store are 17 miles away in Wakefield.

Union River Outpost:

A mile south of the Visitor Center is this three-site rustic campground. Overlooking the Union River, the sites are in a stand of hardwoods and pine and well secluded from South Boundary Road. Unfortunately, Union River could be filled any night of the summer due to it close proximity to M-107. Facilities include vault toilets, fire rings, and tables, but there is no hand pump or any other safe water source. Nearby are the posted trailheads for Union Mine Trail and Union Spring Trail that lead into the interior of the Porkies.

Lost Creek Outpost:

Located 7 miles along South Boundary Road is Lost Creek Campground. The facility is situated across the road from the trailhead of the Lost Lake Trail and has three semi-open sites near Lost Creek but not directly on it. There are fire rings, tables, and vault toilets but no source of safe water.

White Pine Extension:

Continuing west along South Boundary Road, White Pine Extension is reached in 10 miles from M-107 and is the least likely to be filled of the three outlying campgrounds. The outpost campground lies near the Little Iron River and features eight sites in a wooded area. Like the others, White Pine has tables, fire rings, and vault toilets but no water source. The nearest trailheads are on the Summit Peak access road 1.5 miles west on South Boundary Road.

Big Carp River Six-Bunk Cabin

Organization Campground:

Located off M-107, just east of South Boundary Road, is an organization campground for groups. There are no minimum requirements for the number of people in a group, and it is used on a first-come, first-serve basis. The facility consists of two group sites, each capable of holding roughly 25 people. There are vault toilets and tables but no source of water. Water can be obtained at Union Bay Campground. Interested groups should call the park headquarters in advance of their trip for more information.

Cabins

Perhaps one of the most unique aspects of Porcupine Mountains Wilderness State Park is the trailside cabins. Other parks have cabins, even some you have to hike into, but none have as many that are accessed from such an extensive network of foot trails as the Porkies. This may be the only place in the Midwest where you can put together a legitimate three or four-day backpacking trip with every night spent in a different cabin rather than a tent.

The cabins range in size from two to eight bunks and access could be a five minute walk from the road or a four-mile trek. The units are rented from May through the firearm deer season which runs from November 16-30. Three of them, however, are especially built for winter use and are rented out year-round (See chapter 11).

Facilities include bunks with mattresses, wood-burning stove, table, chairs, pots and pans, plates and eating utensils, saw and axe. There is also a log book in each cabin that makes for some entertaining reading. Cabin users should bring sleeping bags or other bedding, food, towels, either a lantern or candles for lighting, dish soap, and toilet paper. A small backcountry stove is also highly recommend for cooking as preparing meals on the wood stoves takes a great deal more time and down wood can be scarce during the summer in some areas. You will need to either boil or filter your water for drinking or cooking purposes as there are no hand pumps in the backcountry.

Some cabin users rent one unit and then use it as a base for dayhikes deeper into the backcountry, but park officials say the majority of people rent several cabins and then spend their visit hiking from one to the next. All of this, of course, requires careful planning and advance reservations.

Buckshot:

This four-bunk is a scenic 2.5 mile hike in from the Lake Superior trailhead on M-107… and a steep hike back out as you have to climb from lake level back up the Escarpment. The cabin is situated just off the shoreline, 30 yards from the water, and its north windows provide a view of the lake itself. A day can be spent hiking the Lake Superior Trail to Lone Rock while the sunsets on a clear evening are spectacular anywhere along the shoreline.

Big Carp River Six-Bunk:

This is one of the largest and most scenic cabins in the park, with one row of windows overlooking Lake Superior and another with a view of the Big Carp River. It's a beautiful 9.6-mile trek from Lake of the Clouds Scenic Area along the Big Carp River Trail. The quickest way to reach the cabin is to begin on the Pinkerton Trail off of South Boundary Road, but that's still a walk of 4 miles. Outside, a bench overlooks a bridge and a large pool in the river where more than one person has enjoyed their morning coffee. The mouth of the Big Carp River is a busy place on a summer evening, however, due to the backcountry campsites and two other cabins in the area.

Big Carp River Four-Bunk:

Up the river and slightly more secluded is this four-bunk unit on a bluff along the west bank. It is near the start of the Cross Trail and is situated directly above some deep pools where salmon can be seen gathering in the fall.

Kaug Wudjoo Lodge

Named from an Ojibwa phrase meaning "place of the crouching porcupine," the most stunning accommodations in Porcupine Mountains Wilderness State Park is Kaug Wudjoo (kahg-WAD-jiw) Lodge. The four-bedroom home was built shortly after the park opened in 1945 as a residence for the park manager and was totally refurbished in 2005.

Set on the shores of Lake Superior, the lodge features hard maple flooring, a large stone fireplace, cedar beds in each bedroom, and a handcrafted, eight-foot long, white pine dining table that accents the lodge's rustic décor. A 16-foot picture window allows guest to view the Great Lake while modern amenities include a fully-equipped kitchen, one-and-half baths, and a laundry room.

Kaug Wudjoo accommodates 12 people and is rented by the week for $1,225, plus an $8 non-refundable reservation fee. To reserve the lodge or for more information call the Porcupine Mountains Wilderness State Park headquarters (906-885-5275) Monday through Friday, from 8 a.m. to 4:30 p.m. EST.

Who needs to rough it? The Kaug Wudjoo Lodge overlooks Lake Superior near the Union Bay Campground and can be rented out by the week. (Michigan DNR photo)

Lake Superior:

The third cabin at the mouth of the Big Carp River is a four-bunk unit that is a short walk west of the bridge along the Lake Superior Trail. This cabin is more shrouded in trees and lacks the clear view of Lake Superior or Big Carp River which makes the other two so popular. All three are the farthest from a trailhead of any in the park, a 4-mile hike along the Pinkerton and Lake Superior Trails.

Little Carp:

Perched on a steep hill above the mouth of the river is this four-bunk cabin. Little Carp is a mile west of the Big Carp River and 3 miles from South Boundary Road at the end of the Pinkerton Trail. With a full pack on, the hill can be a scramble at times, especially in the rain. Once at the cabin you're greeted with a partial view of the river below but none of Lake Superior through the surrounding trees.

Speakers:

This four-bunk cabin is located near the junction between the Lake Superior Trail and Speakers Trail. It is a rugged 2.5-mile hike in from Presque Isle Campground or a fairly easy mile from South Boundary Road. Built in 1977, Speakers has a scenic setting along the edge of a bluff overlooking both the Great Lake and the mouth of Speakers Creek. Outside you'll find a fire ring and benches positioned to take advantage of the view. Nearby by is sandy stretch of shoreline for those brave enough to take a dip in frigid Lake Superior.

Greenstone Falls:

Built in 1948 and renovated after a fire in 1990, Greenstone Falls is a four-bunk cabin that overlooks Little Carp River while its namesake cascade is just upstream. The cabin is 5.5 miles from Mirror Lake, 6.4 miles from the mouth of the Big Carp River, via the Little Carp River Trail, or an easy mile walk from the end of Little Carp River Road off South Boundary Road. The only drawback of the unit is its location right on Little Carp River Trail, a popular route during the summer.

Section 17:

One of the most secluded cabins in the park, Section 17 is a four-bunk unit on the south side of Little Carp River, just across from where Cross Trail joins Little Carp River Trail. It is 5.5 miles up the Little Carp River Trail from Lake Superior or 1.5 miles if you follow the spur off of South Boundary. Originally built as a ranger patrol cabin, Section 17 sits on a low bluff overlooking the river in a stand of hardwoods whose colors are stunning in the late September. A half mile upstream is the Greenstone Falls.

The Crosscut Cabin is a warming shelter in the winter but in the summer can be rented out for overnight stays. The cabin is adjacent to the park's mountain biking trail near Union Spring.
(Michigan DNR photo)

Lily Pond:

Lily Pond is another four-bunk cabin off by itself in a somewhat secluded location in the park. Lily Pond faces a foot bridge over the Little Carp River and the pond that it flows through for a scenic setting. There is a canoe that can be used in the small lake though fishing is marginal at best. The cabin lies on the Little Carp River Trail, but the quickest route to it is a 3-mile hike along Lily Pond Trail from Summit Peak Road.

Mirror Lake Eight-Bunk:

Mirror Lake Eight-Bunk is the classic log cabin in the wilderness and was the first to be built by the park staff in 1946. This eight-bunk unit reminds most users of a hunting lodge in the mountains both for its size and its perch above the lake. It is roomy inside, while outside there is a bench where the sunrise over Mirror Lake can be enjoyed. The cabin also comes with two rowboats for use on the lake. The only drawback is Mirror Lake Trail which runs right past the front door. Envious backpackers are forever peeking inside. The cabin is a rugged 4-mile trek from the Lake of the Clouds Escarpment or a shorter and slightly easier 2.5-mile hike from Summit Peak Road on South Mirror Lake Trail.

Mirror Lake Four-Bunk:

Just to the west is this four-bunk cabin, the second of three units on the north shore of the lake. The log structure is not perched on the edge of the lake like the eight-bunk unit but still has a view of the shoreline and is equipped with a rowboat. The Mirror Lake Trail also runs in front of the cabin.

Lake of the Clouds Cabin on the park's famous lake.

Mirror Lake Two-Bunk:

The third cabin on Mirror Lake is actually positioned above the water on a ridge, away from hikers passing through. Mirror Lake Two-Bunk is another ranger cabin converted for renting and is the smallest in the park. It's a tight squeeze for even two people, thus its nickname: the Honeymoon Suite. Its location is a much more secluded spot to spend the evening even if you do have to scramble down the slope to enjoy the lake. A canoe is provided with the unit so it is easier to haul it up and down.

Lake of the Clouds:

This is a four-bunk cabin situated only a few feet from the shore of the park's most noted natural treasure. Hardwoods surround the unit, but from its windows and bench there is a clear view of the water and the ridges that enclose it. Lake of the Clouds is a hike of less than a mile from the Escarpment viewing area along the North Mirror Lake Trail, but a steep climb back out. The cabin comes with a boat and, needless to say, is an extremely popular unit.

Union River:

This eight-bunk cabin is one of three "winter units," the reason for the cement floor, but it is still a charmer. It's located off the Union Spring Trail, a mile from the trailhead, and overlooks a spot where the Union River swirls past a rocky bluff. The cabin features a wide L-shaped kitchen. Because it's insulated for winter, the room warms up fast once the stove is lit and stays warm throughout the night.

Whitetail:

The second winter unit is located on Lake Superior and is accessed from Deer Yard Trail, primarily a cross country ski route. It's a mile hike in from the trailhead just west of the downhill ski area on M-107. The design is similar to Union River, but Whitetail, an eight-bunk cabin, is on a bluff overlooking Lake Superior in a forest of young hardwoods and paper birch. The view is excellent, and the picnic table and fire pit are angled to take full advantage of the watery horizon.

Gitche Gumee:

This cabin was built for both winter use and physically impaired visitors. It is on the south side of M-107 before South Boundary Road. The trail to Gitchee Gumee, a five-minute walk from where you park the car, is handicapped accessible as is the vault toilet outside. There are no other foot trails nearby.

White Birch:

The park has three warming shelters for cross country skiers in the winter that are rented May through November as small cabins. White Birch is half mile from M-107 along the Superior Loop, a mountain bike and hiking trail passes in front of it. Nearby is the Lake Superior shoreline. The nine-by-ten-foot cabin sleeps two and includes mattresses, kitchen utensils, a wood stove, and a vault toilet.

Crosscut:

Another small two-person cabin, Crosscut is a 2.5-mile hike or mountain bike ride from the Union Spring trailhead on South Boundary Road. The cabin is located in a stand of aspen and birch near Union Spring.

Log Camp Cabin, used as a warming shelter in the winter for cross country skiers.

Log Camp Cabin:

This cabin is also along the mountain bike trails or is a 2.2 mile trek in from the Shingle Mill Parking Area, a quarter mile south of the park headquarters on South Boundary Road. The cabin is reached via River Trail and Log Camp Trail and is less than half mile from the panoramic views of East Vista. Log Camp sleeps four, and along with bunks, a vault toilet and kitchen utensils are supplied with drinking water.

The Lost Creek Yurt is only a half mile hike in from South Boundary Road on Lost Lake Trail. (Michigan DNR photo)

Yurts

More trailside accommodations arrived at the Porkies in 2006 when the park added its first yurt, a sturdy, tent-like structure that originated in central Asia. The popularity of the year-round structure led the park to add three more. The yurts measure 16 feet in diameter and are equipped with four bunks, cooking and eating utensils, a wood stove, and an axe and bow saw. Running water and electricity are not provided, but an outhouse is located nearby. Like campsites and cabins, the yurts are reserved through the Michigan State Park Central Reservation system.

Little Union River:

The park's first yurt is located in a second-growth forest of maple and oak along its namesake river. During the winter the yurt is a 7.5-mile ski via the groomed cross country ski trails of Nonesuch, River and Union Spring or a 3-mile trek beginning with the ungroomed interpretive trail from the Park Headquarters (See chapter 11). In the summer you can reach it within a half mile from the Union Spring Trailhead along South Boundary Road.

West Vista:

Perched on the lofty ridge of the downhill ski slopes, West Vista is a beautiful place to spend the night in the summer and a stunning one in the winter when bare trees give way to mountainous views. Less than a half mile away is the West Vista viewing point that looks over Lake of the Clouds. During the winter the yurt can be reached utilizing the triple chair lift or can be a 5-mile ski along groomed trails that includes a stiff climb up Double Trail. In the summer the yurt is 2-mile hike in via Overlook Trail. Potable water is provided at this yurt from May through October.

Lost Creek:

The park's most unusual winter adventure is a wilderness trek to Lost Creek Yurt (See chapter 11). During the summer the yurt is easy to reach, a half-mile hike up the Lost Lake Trail to a spur across Lost Creek. In the winter snowshoers and backcountry skiers embark on a 6-mile trek from the park headquarters to the four-person tent structure that includes 3.6 miles along a flagged route that is packed but not groomed. The yurt is situated in a beautiful stand of old growth hemlock and maple within 100 feet of the creek.

Union Bay:

The newest yurt is located near the Union Bay Campground. During the summer the yurt is reached from a 75-yard path that is handicapped accessible, putting users within easy walking distance to showers, modern restrooms, and Lake Superior. In the winter you begin at the Deer Yard Trailhead on M-107 and ski or snowshoe in 0.5 mile.

Reservations

Reservations can be made in advance at the two largest campgrounds, Union Bay and Presque Isle, through the Michigan State Park Central Reservation Service (800-44-PARKS; *www. midnrreservations.com*). You can reserve campsites six months from your date of arrival and online can see how many sites are open and which ones. Sites in the park's smaller campgrounds, Union River Outpost, Lost Creek, and White Pine Extension, cannot be reserved in advance and are filled on a first-come-first-serve basis.

The Central Reservation System also handles reservations for rustic cabins and yurts and begins booking these facilities a year in advance. Advance reservations include a small booking fee as well as a nightly site fee and can be paid either by mailing a check or with a Master Card or Visa credit card.

Union River Cabin

Chapter Four
WILDERNESS FISHING

Twang!

Graphite, in the form of a six-foot rod strapped to my backpack, met green wood in the form of a young beech sapling, and for a split second they were intertwined with each other. My next step separated this composite and wooden arch in the middle the trail, leaving them both vibrating and me cursing under my breath.

Why didn't I take the time to find my four-piece trail rod?

No salmon trip ever began like this for me. Not only was I hiking to the river, as opposed to driving, but I was carrying a 40-pound backpack so I could spend a few nights deep inside Porcupine Mountains Wilderness State Park. Then there was the tip of my rod, getting mixed up in every branch along the narrow trail.

Twang!

All this to reach the Big Carp, a river few anglers think of when the annual spawning runs of chinook and coho are heating up in Great Lakes tributaries. That's because you tend to twang your rods hiking in. Yet the run up the Big Carp offers something no other river in the state can do in the fall: To catch salmon and later steelhead in the state's most scenic setting. To fish a pool without being elbow to elbow with 20 other anglers along the bank. To fish all day and not see a single driftboat. To catch a salmon in the solitude of the wilderness.

Although rarely considered an angler's final destination, there are fishing opportunities throughout the Porkies. When you visit, by all means, pack a rod, but also be aware of the limitations that wilderness imposes on anglers. And that begins with the realization that most of the park's fishing opportunities are hike-in experiences.

The park does maintain an improved boat launch in the Union Bay campground, and anglers use it to troll the deep water fishery of Lake Superior. Lake trout is the predominate species caught, and the waters just a few miles off the park offer some of the best lake trout fishing in the area, especially in June and July. Anglers also troll for steelhead, salmon, and brown trout.

All fishing beyond that, however, is done in a backcountry setting which includes a ban on outboard or electric motors, even if you have a back strong enough to carry one in. Fishing the handful of lakes within the park from shore can be rewarding but also somewhat restrictive due to the lack of shoreline trail. If your sole desire is to fish, either pack in waders or, better yet, carry in a boat. Some cabins come with a rowboat (See chapter 3) while a canoe can be portaged into Lake of the Clouds. To fish any of the other three, your best bet is a belly boat as none of the lakes are so large they can't be covered in a float tube.

Angler is caught in an April snowstorm while fishing for steelhead. Big Carp River in the Porcupine Mountains offers perhaps the ultimate wilderness steelhead adventure in Michigan. Just remember to pack the longjohns.

Seasons, tackle regulations, and limits that apply to the rest of Michigan are in effect in the state park. All anglers over the age of 12 must purchase a Michigan fishing license. Here is a brief overview of the fishing opportunities in the Porkies:

Fishing for smallmouth bass in Lake of the Clouds
in the rowboat from the Lake of the Clouds Cabin.

Lake of the Clouds:

The 300-acre lake has a maximum depth of 15 feet. Lake of the Clouds is the largest in the park and probably the most photographed lake anywhere in the state. In all this scenic splendor, what is often overlooked is the lake's outstanding smallmouth bass fishery. Most bass range from 13 to 16 inches though an occasional 20-inch, five-pound bass is hooked. In order to protect the fishery, special catch-and-release, artificial-lures-only regulations have been placed on the lake. Anglers work a variety of rigs (jigs with twister tails, countdown crankbaits, and Mepps spinners) bouncing them along rocky drop-offs on the north side of the lake or running them pass deadheads and old beaver lodges near the shore.

Lake of the Clouds is a mile descent from the Escarpment Overlook parking lot at the end of M-107 and close enough to justify hauling a canoe in for a day. Just remember, it's a steep climb out. The four-bunk cabin on the lake's north shore also has a rowboat. Catch and release is strongly recommended throughout the park but especially in Lake of the Clouds.

Where's the Impoundment?

In the 1960s a dam was built across Union River just downstream of Union Spring, and the result was a large pond reached after a 1.5-mile hike from South Boundary Road. Known simply as the Impoundment, fisheries biologists began stocking it with brook trout, and at first the species thrived in the cold clear water that Union Spring was pumping out.

Gradually the Union Impoundment began filling in with silt, the curse of most impoundments, and the trout struggled to survive. Eventually the stocking program was discontinued. When a drawn down was conducted in 2007, workers discovered the dam was structurally damaged and beginning to fail.

Today the Impoundment is gone and the dam is slated to be totally removed by 2011. After the structure is dismantled, biologists can begin to rehabilitate this segment the Union River into the cold water fishery that it once was. Then maybe the brook trout will return in healthy numbers and backpackers can once cast a line in hopes of catching dinner.

Mirror Lake:

This 83-acre lake has a maximum depth of 40 feet and from 1986-96 was stocked with brook trout that struggled to reach legal size. Since 1997 the lake has been stocked with splake, a cross between brook trout and lake trout. The hatchery-raised trout range from six to eight inches in length when they are stocked and at that size have an excellent survival rate. At times, especially in the spring, the fishing can be excellent in Mirror Lake with many splake ranging from 14 to more than 20 inches in length. Due to the three cabins and the backcountry campsites, the lake experiences the heaviest fishing pressure in the park.

The lake is a 2.5 to 4-mile hike in depending on which trailhead you depart from. All three cabins on the lake are equipped with a boat, the Mirror Lake Eight-Bunk Cabin with two boats.

Lily Pond:

This small lake in the southwest corner of the park has a surface of 12 acres and a depth of 11 feet. Lily Pond is not stocked, but the streams and creeks that feed it contain natural brook trout that migrate into Lily Pond. The lake is a 3-mile hike in and there is a rowboat at the cabin.

Lost Lake:

Situated in the southeast corner of the park is Lost Lake, the smallest of the lakes and a 2-mile walk in from its trailhead on South Boundary Road. The lake is not stocked and receives little if any fishing pressure during the summer.

Big Carp River:

Unquestionably the most remote river in the park, the Big Carp is probably also the most difficult to reach salmon run in the state. Beginning near Lake of the Clouds, the Big Carp flows entirely in the Porcupine Mountains, miles from any road. Several trails lead to its mouth, but the shortest hike in is still a 4-mile trek via the Pinkerton and Lake Superior trails.

Salmon begin appearing in mid-September and peak by early October when, as one park manager put it, "Some pools are so loaded you can practically walk across them." In streams, salmon are taken on spinners, spoons, plugs, spawn, even flies, and single eggs with rods and six-pound test line.

April is the prime month for taking a spring steelhead in the park though in recent years the runs have been poor. These are wild steelhead as the rivers are not planted and occasionally the fish range from four to six pounds. Anglers turn to #2 Mepps spinners as well as spawn while fly fishermen have an excellent opportunity to use nymphs and attractors on the Big Carp to hook into the spawning trout.

The river can be easily waded as most of its lower portion consists of pools and rapids with good stretches of gravel in between. The upper portion of the Big Carp, above Correction Line Trail, has some of the best brook trout waters in the park but be prepared to buck a lot brush to reach the desirable pools.

Little Carp River:

It may be labeled a river on the map, but the Little Carp is more like a mountain steam in many places. This river also attracts a steelhead run in the spring with anglers catching fish that range up to four pounds. Farther upstream the Little Carp has pools and pockets of brook trout. Overall it is fished much harder than the Big Carp due to its proximity to South Boundary Road. It is a

3-mile hike to the river mouth along the Pinkerton Trail although the better brook trout section, near Greenstone Falls, is only a mile hike in.

Presque Isle River:

This spectacular river on the west side of the park receives the most attention from steelheaders, but its run is short as Manabezho Falls stop the trout from moving farther upstream. Most anglers arrive to surf fish the river mouth where they spike their rods into the ground and work rigs of cut spawn or spoons.

Farther upriver, beyond South Boundary Road, there is a brook trout fishery to enjoy. The river mouth is a short descent from the Presque Isle picnic area at the end of County Road 519. To reach the best brook trout pools, you are on your own through brush, though the county road parallels it closely in the beginning.

Other Streams:

The Union River has a steelhead run of its own in the spring and parts of the river can be reached by the ski trail that parallels it after crossing South Boundary Road. Upper portions of it can be fished for brook trout.

Naturally the best brook trout fishing in the park are in the hardest spots to reach. You can spend an adventurous afternoon bushwhacking up the more remote streams searching for that hidden pool with a 12-inch brookie. Good streams to search include the Upper Carp River which can be accessed 2.5 miles up Lost Lake Trail or Little Iron River that flows near White Pine Extension and Lost Creek outpost campgrounds.

Union Bay:

Fishing can also be very good in Union Bay during the spring and fall both for surf anglers and those with a boat set up for trolling. Anglers tend to target lake trout and salmon in the fall and steelhead and brown trout in the spring. Anglers trolling spoons along the shoreline on planer boards do especially well with brown trout in the spring.

One of the many waterfalls along the Big Carp River.

Chapter Five
THE WATERFALLS

She stopped along the Big Carp River at the end of a long day that began by shouldering her 35-pound backpack at the Lake of the Clouds Overlook. Now she figured she was only a mile or so from her destination on Lake Superior when she noticed the sign.

It read "Bathtub Falls."

She looked around and missed it at first. Not surprising. The second half of Big Carp River Trail is a pathway of cascades from thundering Shining Cloud Falls to many that are unnamed but still delightful drops in the current. Bathtub Falls was not like any of them. It was little more than a splash in the river's whitewater run to the Great Lake.

Then she noticed the pools and flat boulders nearby, and suddenly her feet were aching from miles of rugged trail and her shoulders were throbbing from a backpack with too much gear. She dropped the pack, untied her boots, and stripped off two pairs of socks. Her feet were free at last, and she eased them into the swirling cold water of the river.

Ahhhhh! A jacuzzi in the middlle of the wilderness! She lay back on the warm rock, stared at the blue sky above her and thought, "nicest falls I've seen all day."

Some places in Michigan might have bigger and more impressive waterfalls, but no state park can boast a larger collection of cascades than the Porcupine Mountains. Within the park there are more than a dozen named falls, numerous others that aren't, and after any hard rain there will be falling water in every creek and stream. Most of the cascades are only in the backcountry and can only be enjoyed by those who leave their cars and take to the trails on foot.

Waterfall lovers, intent on seeing as many as possible, would do well to include in their itinerary the Big Carp River Trail, Little Carp River Trail, and the East-West River Trails along the Presque Isle. What follows is a thumbnail stretch of the major falls in the parks. Some are spectacular and labeled on every map while the beauty of others is seen only by those with aching feet and throbbing shoulders.

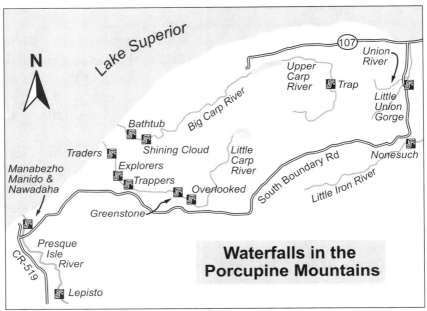

Manabezho Falls:

There are four named cascades on Presque Isle River within the park, and three of them can be viewed by hiking the East or West River Trail. The swing bridge near the Presque Isle picnic area provides an excellent view of the river's final drop into Lake Superior where the spinning action of the current is so strong it has carved half circles in the bed rock and along the shoreline.

Following the West Trail boardwalk upriver, you reach Manabezho Falls in about 200 yards, the most impressive section of whitewater in the Presque Isle. Here, the 150-foot-wide river drops more than 20 feet over a rock ledge in a thunder of copper color water and mist.

Manido Falls:

Another 100 yards upriver is Manido Falls, which drops a total of 25 feet, first over a series of declining rock steps and then a ledge where the water slides over large sections of shale. The falls can be seen from both sides of the river, but farther along West Trail there is an observation platform extending from the riverbank.

Nawadaha Falls:

Closest to South Boundary Road is Nawadaha Falls, a cascade that drops 15 feet over a series rock steps. The falls are easier to see from the East Trail than the west side where you need to leave the path to get a good look at it.

Overlooked Falls:

There are five named falls along the Little Carp River with the first two reached in less than a mile from the end of Little Carp River Road. Overlooked is a mere 100 feet from where you park the car, and it's actually a pair of cascades with a total drop 10 feet, with the second falls split in the middle by a huge rock boulder.

Greenstone Falls along Little Carp River Trail.

Greenstone Falls:

Several more small falls are passed along the trail and then 0.75 mile from the trailhead, just along the Little Carp River Trail toward the cabins, you reach Greenstone Falls. Set in a small gorge, the cascade features a 15-foot wide veil that tumbles six feet down a series of rock steps and small boulders.

Explorers and Trappers Falls:

This pair of falls is located close together along the Little Carp River Trail, 4 miles from Little Carp Road or 2.5 miles from the trailhead along Lake Superior. If heading towards the lake, you pass Trappers first, where the 12-foot wide Little Carp River forms a veil as it tumbles over a rock embankment an impressive waterslide, then fords the river to quickly arrive at Explorers, more rapids than cascade.

Traders Falls:

The final falls are a half mile from the Lake Superior shoreline. The Little Carp River departs along the east side bank, opposite the cabin, and immediately climbs a gorge. You can see Traders Falls just before the trail descends to the river bank.

Shining Cloud Falls:

In the northern half of the Big Carp River Trail, after its junction with Correction Line Trail, you pass almost a dozen waterfalls beginning with one of the most impressive cascades in the park. Shining Cloud is also the highest in the Porkies at almost 800 feet and is reached 1.5 miles from the Lake Superior Trailhead or 7.5 miles from the Lake of the Clouds Overlook. The cascade is set in a deep, rocky gorge and is a 30 to 35-foot drop split by a large rocky outcropping before spilling into a large pool.

Bathtub Falls:

From Shining Cloud north along the river you pass a dozen cascades, all unnamed, but several have a drop of six feet or more with inviting pools at their base. This magnificent stretch of whitewater, where the Big Carp River tumbles down to the lower level of Lake Superior, ends with Bathtub Falls, a series of small ledges and little pools.

Trap Falls:

The best cascade in the east half of the park is Trap Falls. These can be reached at 2.5 miles on the Government Peak Trail from M-107 or 4.5 miles if you begin on the Union Spring Trail. Situated in an impressive gorge area, the falls feature a 15 to 20-foot drop along a narrow rock slide and end in the most inviting pool in the park. The area is shaded by towering pines, and there's a bench overlooking the river to rest your feet and enjoy this scenic spot.

Little Union Gorge And Union River Falls:

There are several small falls in the Little Union Gorge area and along the Union River that can be accessed from the Union Mine Trail. You have to leave the trail to see the most impressive cascades along the Union River. They are best reached from the iron bridge at Union River Outpost Campground. From the center of the bridge, you can see small falls upstream while a ski/mountain bike trail will take you along the river downstream to view additional drops in the river. The falls on the Little Union River can be very impressive in the spring runoff or after a heavy rain. Most of them can be viewed from the trail.

Nonesuch Falls:

Located on the Little Iron River near the remains of Nonesuch Mine is this 12-foot cascade that is divided by a boulder in the middle. It ends with a seven-foot deep pool before the river continues it journey to Lake Superior. The falls are reached from South Boundary Road 4.3 miles south of M-107. Where South Boundary makes a sharp curve west, the gravel road continues south and in less than a mile reaches the cascade.

Chapter Six

THE LAKE SUPERIOR TRAIL

The longest route in the Porkies is the Lake Superior Trail, a 17.1-mile walk from M-107 to the Presque Isle day-use area. This is one of Michigan's classic footpaths, an extended hike that is as highly regarded as the Greenstone Trail on Isle Royale National Park or the Lakeshore Trail in Pictured Rocks National Lakeshore in its level of wilderness adventure.

The Lake Superior Trail takes you from one side of the state park to the other, winding along the largest body of freshwater in the world and crossing such scenic rivers as the Big Carp, Little Carp, and Presque Isle. It is an avenue through the most remote corner of park's 60,000 acres and provides access to six trailside cabins and 20 backcountry campsites.

This trail allows you to witness Lake Superior's fury on a stormy day or a stunning sunset of oranges and reds when the lake is calm. Hiked in its entirety, the Lake Superior route can leave you with that special sense of having trekked from one corner of the park to the other.

Ironically, few people experience the trail from end to end. Being a point-to-point route, there is a bit of a logistical problem of getting back to a car for any party of hikers who do not arrive in two vehicles. Shuttle transport can be arranged through Porcupine Mountain Outpost (906-885-5612), a concessionaire store located near Union Bay Campground. For $80 per vehicle, the Outpost will follow you out to Presque Isle and then transport you to the start of the Lake Superior Trail on M-107. Most trekkers, however, choose to avoid the additional arrangements and cost by combining a portion of the Lake Superior Trail with another trail to form a loop within the park.

The most common itinerary is to begin at M-107 and to return along Big Carp River Trail, a three-day, 19-mile hike. A slightly longer version would be to include Correction Line and North Mirror Lake trails, a 20-mile trek. Perhaps the longest hike in the park is to return along Little Carp River, Government Peak, and Escarpment trails, a 5-day, 36-mile walk.

To make the following description as useful to the most people as possible, Lake Superior Trail will be outlined from the M-107 trailhead to Big Carp River and then from the Presque Isle trailhead to Big Carp River. The easiest direction to hike is east to west due to the fact that you begin on the Escarpment instead of having to climb it at the end.

Although it never climbs into the ridges that are technically the Porcupine Mountains, the Lake Superior Trail can still be a rugged walk at times, especially the west end where have to you climb in and out of several steep ravines to cross streams. Nor should you expect a view of the Great Lake every step of the way. However, the trail winds close to the lake from Lone Rock to Little Carp River, and in this stretch there are many opportunities to stop and admire the water. Otherwise, you will find the rest of the trail, for the most part, is a path through woods.

Like the rest of the park's trail system, after a hard rain the conditions can get muddy, even sloppy at times, and streams can be difficult to cross. Fortunately, the Lake Superior Trail is not nearly as bad as others due to a major upgrade of the route in the mid-1990s which included installing two miles of boardwalk from one end to the other.

A backpacker checks a trail sign along the Lake Superior trail.

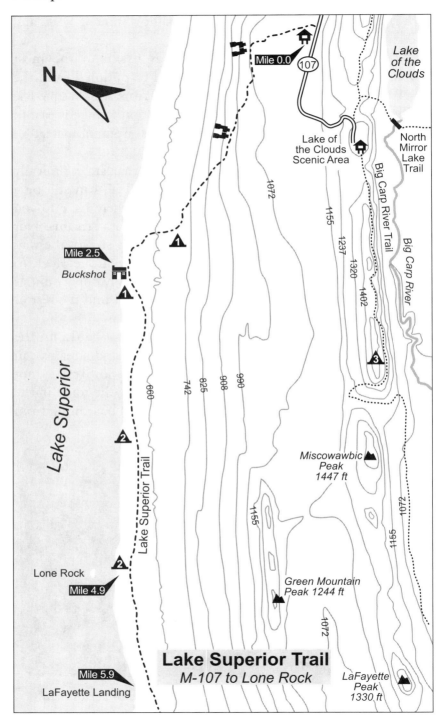

N

Lake
of the
Clouds

Mile 0.0 107

Lake of
the Clouds
Scenic Area

North
Mirror
Lake
Trail

Big Carp River Trail

Big Carp River

1072

1155

1237

1320

1402

Mile 2.5

Buckshot

Lake Superior

Lake Superior Trail

660

742

825

908

990

1155

Miscowawbic
Peak
1447 ft

Lone Rock

Mile 4.9

1072

1155

Green Mountain
Peak 1244 ft

1072

Mile 5.9

LaFayette Landing

Lake Superior Trail
M-107 to Lone Rock

LaFayette
Peak
1330 ft

Lake Superior Trail

M-107 to Big Carp River
    Distance: 2.5 miles to Buckshot Cabin
                  4.9 miles to Lone Rock Campsites
                  5.9 miles to Lafayette Landing
                  9.5 miles to Big Carp River
    Highest Point: 1,220 feet
    Hiking Time: 5 to 7 hours

The eastern trailhead to the Lake Superior Trail is posted along M-107, about a mile east from the road's end at the Escarpment Overlook parking area. The trail departs north from the state road in an old growth forest of pine for a half mile until you gradually ascend to the high point of 1,220 feet and your first view of Lake Superior. From the rocky outcrop you can see Lone Rock just to the west and, if the day is clear, the Apostle Islands off Wisconsin. This is as high as the trail climbs as you never even break 800 feet in the remaining 16 miles.

Lake Superior Trail backpackers crossing the Presque Isle River

The route swings west, follows the ridge briefly to unveil more views of the Great Lake and split log bench then begins dropping to the shoreline. At first the descent is gentle but then becomes a rapid, knee-bending hike downward when the trail swings more to the north. On the way down you pass a backcountry campsite and after a mile, you finally bottom out in an area of young hardwoods. Though you are only a few hundred yards from the lake, it is hard to spot the water through the trees.

The trail swings west, crosses a wet area on a boardwalk, and within a quarter mile you arrive at the spur to Buckshot Landing Cabin, a 2.5 mile walk from M-107. The four-bunk cabin is situated 30 yards from the shoreline with a pleasant view of the lake from its windows. Those who have thoughtfully reserved the unit in advance can throw down the packs and rub their shoulders. Others can choose a backcountry campsite. There is one just west of the cabin and four more posted on the trail before Lone Rock.

The next 6.5 miles to Big Carp River are some of the most level trails in this unleveled park and by far the easiest stretch of the shoreline route. It stays inland from the shoreline for the next 2 miles, far enough so you can't see the water, close enough where you can hear the surf on a windy day. The spur to Lone Rock, a solitary boulder lying a quarter mile offshore, is reached 2.4 miles from Buckshot Landing and 4.9 miles from M-107. Scattered along the trail from the cabin are four more backcountry sites with the last two clustered near the Lone Rock spur. The short spurs to the campsites are marked along the trail and the sites are either within view of the lake or very close to it.

Within 1.7 miles from Lone Rock, the trail swings back towards the shoreline and arrives at a pile of rubble and rocks in a small clearing. One of the park's three Adirondack-style shelters once stood here, but eventually all of them were removed. What remains today is the short path that once provided access to the lake for the shelter dwellers.

To the west the remaining 3 miles to Big Carp River are some of the most delightful stretches of the long route. You quickly break out along the shoreline and stay there for a mile or more. From the middle of the path, you're rewarded with a continuous view of this sea of blue with the waves breaking only a few feet away.

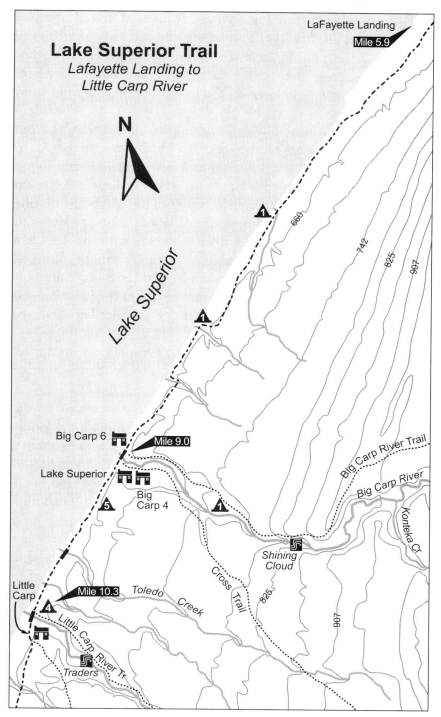

Lake Superior Trail
*Lafayette Landing to
Little Carp River*

N

Lake Superior

LaFayette Landing
Mile 5.9

660

742

825

907

Big Carp 6
Mile 9.0

Lake Superior

5

Big
Carp 4

Big Carp River Trail

Big Carp River

Konteka Cr.

Shining
Cloud

825

Cross Trail

907

Little
Carp
Mile 10.3

Toledo Creek

4

Little Carp River Tr.

Traders

There is a bit of climbing involved at first as the trail traverses the narrow bench that lays between the lake and a low ridge to the southeast. After passing a backcountry campsite, the trail climbs the low ridge and then descends back to the shoreline where another walk-in site is located. You're now roughly a mile from Big Carp River.

The trail climbs the low ridge once more, and 4.6 miles from Lone Rock you emerge on the edge of a bluff above the Big Carp River. The trail quickly descends into a large flat area, arriving at a well-marked junction with Big Carp River Trail near Big Carp Six-Bunk Cabin. The cabin, overlooking the Big Carp River is one of the most picturesque in the park and one of the most popular to reserve. Just before reaching the river, a junction with the Big Carp River Trail is reached. By combining a portion of that route with Correction Line Trail you could reach Mirror Lake in 7 miles.

Lake Superior Trail continues west (right) at the junction and crosses the Big Carp River on a footbridge that lies between two huge boulders with a bench at one end.

Here you can sit and rest those tired toes while viewing the river rippling into the surf of Lake Superior, and if it is September you can watch salmon spawn upstream.

The mouth of the Big Carp River is the farthest point in the park from any road. Break a leg here and it is a loooong 4-mile trek to pavement. It is also one of the most scenic places to spend a night in the park. The large gravel flat, scattered with boulders and driftwood trees washed up during one of Lake Superior's moments of fury, makes an excellent spot to drag out the sleeping pad on a clear evening to watch the sunset.

Once across the bridge you immediately come to the junction with Cross Trail which leads 4.5 miles to Little Carp River Trail and South Boundary Road a mile farther. Just up the trail is the Big Carp River Four-Bunk Cabin in a more secluded spot overlooking a pool in the river.

Continue along Lake Superior Trail for a few yards to reach Lake Superior Cabin, a four-bunk unit tucked away in the trees and out of view for the most part from both the river and the lake. Beyond the cabin a string of five backcountry campsites are marked along the trail, the first only minutes away.

Bridge over Big Carp River
with Big Carp River Six-Bunk Cabin in the background.

If you are continuing on the Little Carp River, Cross Trail, or the second half of the Lake Superior Trail, try to squeeze in a side trip to Shining Cloud Falls. It is a one-way trek of 1.4 miles from the mouth with most of the time spent paralleling scenic Big Carp River until you reach the falls, a stunning sight.

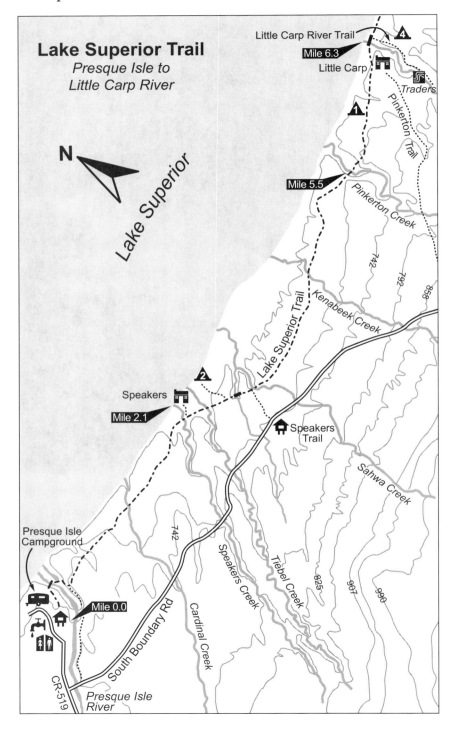

Lake Superior Trail
*Presque Isle to
Little Carp River*

N

Lake Superior

Little Carp River Trail
Mile 6.3
Little Carp

4

Traders

Pinkerton Trail

1

Mile 5.5

Pinkerton Creek

742

792

858

Kenabeek Creek

Lake Superior Trail

2

Speakers
Mile 2.1

Speakers
Trail

Sahwa Creek

Presque Isle
Campground

742

825

907

990

Speakers Creek

Triebel Creek

Cardinal Creek

Mile 0.0

South Boundary Rd

CR-519

Presque Isle
River

The mouth of the Big Carp River at Lake Superior.

Presque Isle Campground to Big Carp River
    Distance: 2.1 miles to Speakers Cabin
        6.3 miles to Little Carp River
        7.6 miles to Big Carp River
    Highest Point: 707 feet
    Hiking Time: 4 to 6 hours

The highest point along the western half of the Lake Superior Trail is only 707 feet reached near Pinkerton Stream, but don't let that deceive you. You do an awful lot of climbing, and descending, along this stretch, and it begins the minute you depart from the backpacker's parking lot near the Presque Isle Campground.

You no sooner lock your car then you are descending along a boardwalk and stairway towards the Presque Isle River, crossing a stretch of whitewater on an impressive swing bridge. A thin peninsula in the mouth of the river lies on the other side where a spur diverts to the Lake Superior shoreline. The main trail descends from the peninsula to what appears to be a dry river channel, and here you carefully climb over layers of slate with tumbling whitewater just over your shoulder. You are only 10 minutes into the trek and already you are overwhelmed by the scenery.

On the east bank of the river, the trail ascends steeply out of the gorge to a posted junction at the top. To the south is the West River Trail, part of a 2-mile loop along the Presque Isle (See chapter 9). Lake Superior Trail continues east, descends in and then out of two ravines, the second time to cross Cardinal Creek a mile from the trailhead. You are never very far from the Great Lake, and there is an occasional glimpse of the water, but the trail stays away from the shoreline until you reach Little Carp River.

At 2.1 miles you arrive at a directional sign, cross Speaker Creek, and then come to the spur to Speakers Cabin, a four-bunk unit on the edge of a bluff overlooking Lake Superior. Speakers is only a mile from South Boundary Road via Speakers Trail, a considerably easier walk than from Presque Isle.

Lake Superior Trail continues its easterly direction and within 0.3 mile crosses Teibel Creek and then arrives at another spur. This side trail heads to the north (left) and within a quarter mile arrives at a pair of backcountry campsites located where eight summer cabins once were.

At the spur the Lake Superior Trail merges into an old forest road and descends to the third branch of Sahwa Creek that is crossed with the help of a narrow vehicle bridge built by the cabin owners. On the other side, the trail quickly arrives at the posted junction with Speakers Trail. South Boundary Road is 0.5 mile south from here, Presque Isle River 2.6 miles to the west, and Little Carp River 3.7 miles east.

The main trail continues to stay away from the lakeshore in a thick forest for the next 3 miles but remains a somewhat level hike, if that is actually possible in this park. You cross two more branches of Sahwa Creek and then Kenabeek Creek 1.5 miles from Speakers Trail. These are not the deep gorges that Cardinal Creek has carved. Nor is it difficult to keep your boots dry... unless a rain storm passes through, then you might have to search for a better ford than what the trail offers.

Crossing the Little Carp River on the Lake Superior Trail.

Not so with Pinkerton Creek, reached 5.5 miles from the Presque Isle trailhead or 3 miles from Speakers Trail. Just before reaching the west edge of gorge, the trail swings close to Lake Superior, and it is easy to cut across at this point to view the water. Then you ascend slightly to the high point of 707 feet to begin a sharp descent of 60 feet to the creek, only to climb out again on the other side.

Beyond Pinkerton, the trail passes a backcountry campsite just before descending to cross another small creek. On the other side you traverse the top of a low ridge and finally come into view of Little Carp River. Here you find yourself standing on the edge of another steep gorge. What impresses most hikers, however, is not the picturesque river and rocky ravine, but the extensive stairway and bridge across them. Just before descending, a trail leads north along the west bank and then makes a steep climb to Little Carp Cabin. The four-bunk cabin sits on a hill with a partial view of the river but none of the lake.

An even better setting for the night is on the east bank where the trail swings past Little Carp River campsites, four numbered tent pads situated in a wooded area with a view of both the river and Lake Superior. There are also a few benches built by other parties and a group fire pit.

The Little Carp River is a major crossing in the park's trail system with a posted junction on each side. On the west bank near the cabin spur is Pinkerton Trail, which reaches South Boundary Road in 2.6 miles. On the east side is Little Carp River Trail, which first departs south then swings east reaching Greenstone Falls in 6.5 miles, Lily Pond in 9 miles, and finally Mirror Lake in 11.8 miles.

On the final 1.3 miles to Big Carp River, the Lake Superior Trail stays exceptionally close to the lakeshore—so close that on a windy day the surf will be crashing only a few yards away. You pass a couple of backcountry campsites and then in a half mile cross a bridge over Toledo Creek, so named to remind us what little Michigan gave up to get the Porkies and the rest the Upper Peninsula. All hikers from Ohio are permitted to sit down at this point and moan.

The trail continues for another 0.8 mile before finally passing the stairway to some backcountry campsites, located up on a bluff. Not far away are three cabins and the mouth of the Big Carp River, one of the most scenic areas in the park. If you are not stopping here for the evening, at least plan for an extended meal break.

What's in your backpack? A meal at the mouth
of the Big Carp River included smoked trout, fine cheeses,
an English hardsauce and wine-in-the-box, minus the box.

Chapter Seven

THE LONG TRAILS

Little Carp River • Big Carp River • Government Peak

Along with the Lake Superior Trail, there are several long routes within the Porcupine Mountains that require a day or more to hike. Little Carp River extends from the Great Lake to Mirror Lake, a 11.8-mile trek. Big Carp River Trail is a 9.6-mile walk from the Escarpment to the mouth of its namesake river, and Government Peak Trail is a 7.3-mile journey from M-107, over the second highest point in the park to a junction with North Mirror Lake Trail, a mile from Mirror Lake.

Big Carp River Trail rivals the Escarpment for panoramic overlooks and provides hikers with an excellent cross-section view of this amazing state park. Little Carp River Trail is also a scenic journey which for the most part follows the small river to its source. Both are often combined with a portion of the Lake Superior Trail to form a two- to four-day adventure.

The natural features along the Government Peak Trail are less outstanding than what is seen on the other two trails, and subsequently the route receives far less foot traffic during the summer. Portions of this trail, especially around Trap Falls, make for delightful hiking, and when combined with North Mirror Lake and Escarpment, Government Peak becomes part of an excellent two- to three-day outing.

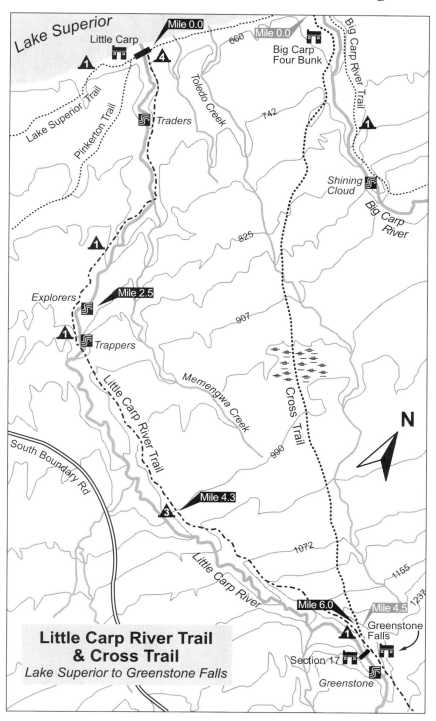

Lake Superior

Little Carp

Mile 0.0

Mile 0.0

Big Carp
Four Bunk

660

742

825

907

990

1072

1155

1237

Toledo Creek

Lake Superior Trail

Pinkerton Trail

Traders

Shining
Cloud

Big Carp River Trail

Big Carp
River

Explorers

Mile 2.5

Trappers

Little Carp River Trail

Memengwa Creek

Cross Trail

N

South Boundary Rd

Mile 4.3

3

Little Carp River

Mile 6.0

Mile 4.5

Greenstone
Falls

Section 17

Greenstone

Little Carp River Trail
& Cross Trail
Lake Superior to Greenstone Falls

A backpacker fords Little Carp River

Little Carp River Trail

Lake Superior to Mirror Lake
  Distances: 6 miles to Cross Trail
           9 miles to Lily Pond
           11.8 miles to Mirror Lake
  Highest Point: 1,560 feet
  Hiking Time: 7 to 9 hours

Little Carp River Trail is the second longest route in the park and one of the most scenic. You can begin near the shores of Lake Superior, elevation 611 feet, and for the most part make a gradual climb to Mirror Lake, which at 1,532 feet is the one of the highest inland lakes in the state. Along the way you pass several waterfalls, three cabins, and a serene little lake in Lily Pond. The trail also connects two sets of backcountry campsites near the mouth of the Little Carp River and on Mirror Lake and passes ten more along the way.

The western half of the trail is free of any steep climbs and fords the river only twice. These bridgeless crossings are usually easy, but immediately after a heavy rainfall you might have to search for a better spot than around the trail, and sometimes you might not be able to ford at all. In June of 1983 a storm dumped 13 inches of rain on the Porkies, and the water along portions of the Little Carp River rose to depths of 30 feet.

Lake Superior to Cross Trail
Distance: 6 miles

Little Carp departs a junction with the Lake Superior Trail on the east side of the river and skirts the edge of the gorge briefly before descending its steep side. You can view Traders Falls on the descent or cut back to the small cascade once you bottom out. From here the trail remains level for a spell, only occasionally climbing into the surrounding bluffs.

This is an extremely scenic portion of the route as you follow the flowing river through stately stands of virgin hemlock and maples. There are ample blazes and other trail signs, and the path is easy to follow. Within 1.5 miles, however, you make your first ford of the day. The ford is well marked, and it is easy to identify the main route on the other side of the river. Keep in mind that there are trails along both shores of much of the river due primarily to anglers searching pools for brook trout.

Now on the west side of the river, you pass a backcountry campsite and then Explorers Falls, reached 2.5 miles from Lake Superior Trail. In 0.3 mile you come to yet another display of falling water, Trappers Falls, a distinctive cascade where the river slides down a wide rock chute. Nearby is a backcountry campsite, while just beyond Trappers Falls you ford the Little Carp a second time.

Back on the east side, the trail for the most part follows the top of the bluffs. Along the way you pass three backcountry campsites, reached 1.5 miles past Trappers Falls. Eventually you climb a low bluff to arrive at the junction with the Cross Trail, 6 miles from Lake Superior Trail. Near the junction is another backcountry campsite and a quarter mile beyond it, you pass a stairway that leads to a foot bridge across the Little Carp River to Section 17 Cabin on the south side. Originally built as a ranger patrol cabin, the four-bunk unit is well secluded from trail traffic and is located on a low bluff overlooking the Little Carp River.

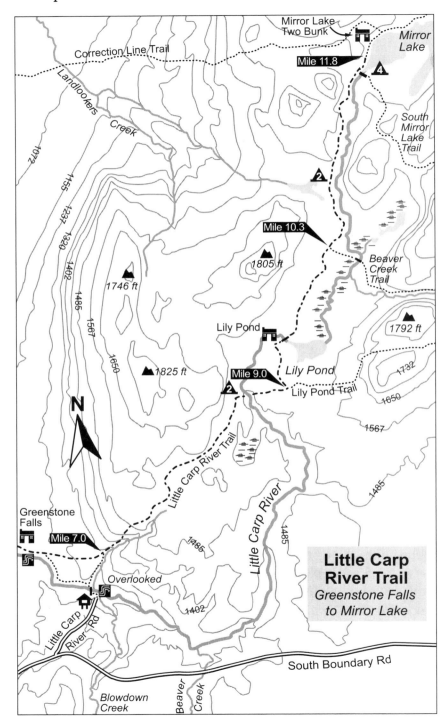

Little Carp
River Trail
*Greenstone Falls
to Mirror Lake*

Greenstone Falls Cabin along the Little Carp River Trail.

Cross Trail to Mirror Lake

Distance: 5.8 miles

The next leg of the trail is the hike to Lily Pond, a good 3-mile trek. A short distance from the Section 17 bridge brings you to the Greenstone Falls Cabin. Recently renovated, the four-bunk unit is within view of the river but not the falls themselves and is located right on the trail. The cascade is posted another 100 yards up the trail. Here the river has formed a veil of water that tumbles 15 feet down a rock embankment in a small gorge, making it a scenic little spot.

Just beyond Greenstone Falls, the trail crosses a bridge over a feeder creek and then arrives at a junction with the access route from Little Carp River Road. A car parking area is only half mile away at this point with South Boundary Road 1.5 miles.

Little Carp River Trail heads east and immediately begins the steepest climb of the route. It is a steady ascent of 160 feet until you top off at the second junction to South Boundary Road. Here an old forest road passes through. Head south on it and South Boundary Road is reached in a mile. The trail continues east and in the next half mile makes a more gentle climb to 1,560 feet, the high point along the route.

You follow the ridge briefly until the trail descends to cross the Little Carp River. Nearby are a pair of backcountry campsites. The Little Carp harbors populations of wild brook trout but is heavily fished in its lower sections. Anglers looking for a little adventure should search the upper portions of the river, accessing it from this crossing.

The trail makes a final climb back to 1,560 feet then descends to a posted junction with Lily Pond Trail. To the south is Lily Pond Trail, which leads 2.5 miles to Summit Peak Road. To the north is Little Carp River Trail that leads through an impressive stand of white pine and in a half mile reaches Lily Pond Cabin, a four-bunk unit surrounded by the towering pines and overlooking the west end of the small lake.

The final leg of the route is the remaining 2.8 miles to Mirror Lake. The trail begins by crossing the Little Carp River where it flows out of the lake. The area is so scenic that the bridge has a bench in the middle of it. The next mile heads northeast along a fairly level route. At times in early spring and late fall, before the leaves obscure the view, you can view the ridge to the southeast and spot several distinctive peaks, including Summit Peak at 1,958 feet.

Within 1.3 miles you pass the posted junction to Beaver Creek Trail, which heads south and in a mile reaches Summit Peak parking area. Little Carp Trail swings more to the north and in the final 1.5 miles skirts its namesake river. The trail then rounds the base of a 1,600-foot high rocky knob that hikers can scramble up for a view of the Mirror Lake area. If you choose not to, the lake will come into view just before you reach the posted junction with South Mirror Lake Trail which heads south to reach Summit Peak Road in 3 miles. Also follow this trail to cross the Little Carp River again and pass the spur to four backcountry campsites situated on a small inlet at the west end. Continue heading east along the lake to pass near the Mirror Lake Two-Bunk Cabin, the junction to the Correction Line Trail and finally Four-Bunk and Eight-Bunk Cabin. Mirror Lake marks the end of the Little Carp River Trail. Continuing on is North Mirror Lake Trail which quickly arrives at a posted spur to three backcountry campsites on the east shore of the lake.

Mirror Lake, one of the highest in Michigan, is a favorite place for many backcountry users to spend an evening. The lake is set among a series of ridges and knobs, like a jewel in the mountains, with towering hemlocks and maples enclosing its shoreline. This place is stunning in late September and very much worthy of its name on any calm day.

The bridge overlooking Lily Pond along the Little Carp River Trail.

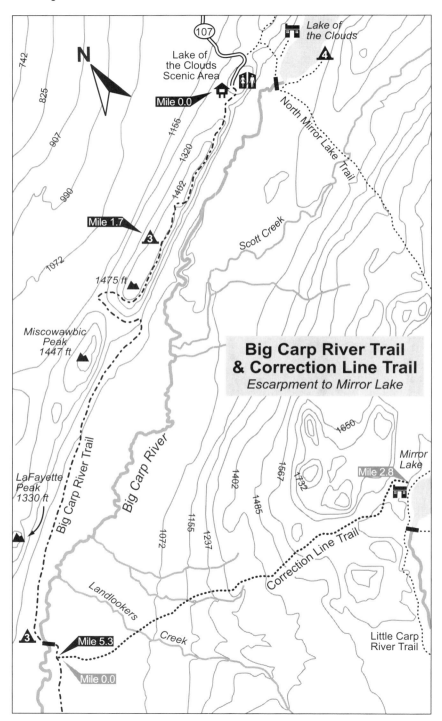

Big Carp River Trail & Correction Line Trail
Escarpment to Mirror Lake

A hiker crosses the Big Carp River along the Big Carp River Trail.

Big Carp River Trail

Escarpment to Lake Superior
  Distances: 5.3 miles to Correction Line Trail
           8.2 miles to Shining Cloud Falls
           9.6 miles to Lake Superior
  Highest Point: 1,447 feet
  Hiking Time: 5 to 7 hours

Truly one of the most incredible hikes in the Porkies, and for that matter anywhere in Michigan, is Big River Carp Trail, a 9.6-mile route that begins at the Lake of the Clouds Overlook and winds it way down to the shores of Lake Superior. The variety of scenery this trail passes through is truly amazing. Along the way there are outstanding alpine-like vistas, stands of virgin hemlock, and a sheer-sided rock gorge filled by Shining Cloud Falls, one of the most spectacular cascades in the Porkies.

The first 2 miles follow the Escarpment with only moderate climbing involved. From there the trail drops off the famous bluff and winds its way into one of the most remote corners of the park. Halfway along the route you'll pass a series of backcountry campsites and at the trail's end there are three cabins near the mouth of the Carp River and more backcountry campsites. Opportunities to set up camp within the gurgle of this wild river are almost unlimited.

A hiker takes a break to enjoy the falling water along the Big Carp River.

Escarpment to Correction Line Trail

Distance: 5.3 miles

From the Lake of the Clouds parking lot at the end of M-107 is the posted trailhead for the route that begins at 1,246 feet. You head west into the woods only to emerge at the first of many scenic views. Within a quarter mile, the trees open up to Lake of the Clouds to the east and Big Carp River valley to the west. The trail then dips back into the wood and begins a steady ascent of 100 feet.

You top out at more than 1,400 feet to break out to a glorious view at the edge of the Escarpment. Here, Lake of the Clouds is a body of water in the distance while the valley heads west and on the horizon you can make out ridges and distinct peaks that lie outside the park. In the next mile, the trail follows the edge of this bluff, passing one spectacular view after another until arriving at a semi-open area. At 1.5 miles into the trek, you can stand on the edge of a rock cliff and peer down a sheer drop to the Big Carp River in the valley below, a stunning sight. Or you can gaze west along the ridge where beyond a gap in the cliff is Miscowawbic Peak in the foreground and 2 miles away LaFayette Peak, marking one end of the Escarpment. There are three backcountry campsites nearby, and it's easy to understand why they were placed here. This is a beautiful spot to set up a tent.

You resume following the bluff briefly then begin the long descent to the floor of the valley. It's a half mile descent, sharp at first but gentle most of the way as you drop from the high point of the day of 1,447 feet to less than 1,100 feet. Along the way you move from a beech/maple forest to a stand of stately hemlock.

Once in the valley, the trail continues southwest through the forest along the base of the Escarpment but remains fairly level and surprisingly dry—not the mud bath North Mirror Lake Trail can become. Even on the hottest day, it is cool and dark in the stand of hemlock where the fallen trunks, many of them victims of the 1953 tornado, are carpeted with bright green moss. At 3.5 miles you appear on the edge of a low rise, skirt it briefly then make a quick descent from hemlock into a forest of beech and maple.

The walk down the valley remains level for a mile, and within a half mile the trail begins passing a series of three backcountry campsites before breaking out at the Big Carp River for the first time a little more than 5 miles from the Lake of the Clouds trailhead. A bridge allows you to cross a 15- to 20-yard-wide river with a gentle flowing current that swirls through an occasional pool. Anglers would do well to drop their packs and scout the Big Carp up stream for brook trout.

From the bridge you quickly emerge where an Adirondack shelter use to be located that inscribed on the door was "Porcupine Hilton" and underneath "World Famous Firm Beds." The junction with Correction Line Trail is well posted and just down the trail or 5.3 miles from the trailhead. From here Mirror Lake is 2.8 miles east and a 600-foot climb along the Correction Line Trail. Lake Superior is 4.3 miles to the west on the Big Carp River Trail.

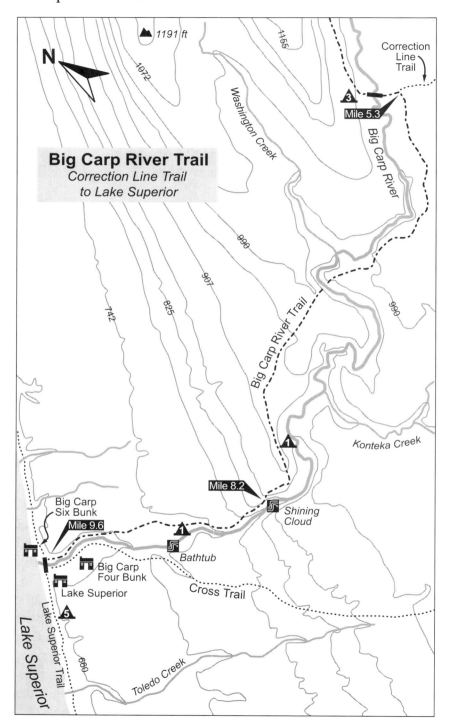

1191 ft

N

Correction
Line
Trail

Big Carp River Trail
*Correction Line Trail
to Lake Superior*

Washington Creek

Big Carp River

3
Mile 5.3

Big Carp River Trail

Konteka Creek

1

Mile 8.2

Shining
Cloud

Big Carp
Six Bunk
Mile 9.6

1

Bathtub

Big Carp
Four Bunk

Lake Superior

Cross Trail

Lake Superior Trail

5

Toledo Creek

Lake Superior

Correction Line Trail to Lake Superior

Distance: 4.3 miles

Continuing toward the lakeshore, Big Carp River Trail dips into a low-lying area, crosses a wet area, and then ascends the bluffs above the river. On the high ground, you follow the river for the next mile as the trail weaves through pines and hemlocks and swings past views of the water. It is another scenic stretch of Big Carp River Trail, but it ends when you descend to ford the river. Normally the crossing is easy, but this is one spot where heavy rains or April's runoff can make it a challenge to cross.

On the other side, the trail immediately makes a steep ascent up the shoreline bluff and then leaves the river as the Big Carp swings towards Lake Superior. This stretch, muddy at times but level, makes an easy stroll through another impressive stand of hemlock. Within 2 miles from the junction with the Correction Line Trail, you return to the Big Carp at the edge of a steep gorge and follow it until you are staring upriver at Shining Cloud Falls.

Many feel the falls are the most spectacular in the park. Actually, Shining Cloud is a pair of cascades that make a 30 to 35-foot drop and are enclosed on one side by stone walls. You can hike down to the thundering water, but take caution as it is a very steep drop. Nearby is a backcountry campsite.

The trail descends from the gorge to skirt the river itself and then for the next 0.5 mile you pass almost a dozen cascades and a backcountry campsite. Some are small, but four of them have drops of more than 6 feet that end in deep pools. Downstate they would be the centerpiece of a state park, but here they are so commonplace they are unnamed and left off the park maps. Less than a mile from departing Shining Cloud you come to an area where Big Carp River levels out at a spot posted "Bathtub Falls." The falls are really a series of one-foot drops and pools. It's so close to the end of a long day, however, that more than one backpacker has soaked his weary feet in this natural ice-cold jacuzzi.

Originally the trail at this point crossed the river and merged into the Cross Trail. A few trail signs still mark the way, but now the route leads you away from the river and makes a steep climb via a series of switchbacks up a river bluff. You top off to one more panorama where far below is the Big Carp River flowing past you and on the horizon you can view Lake Superior for the first time.

For the remaining half mile you hug the edge of the bluff and then descend to Big Carp River Six-Bunk Cabin near the mouth of the river. This is one of the most scenic spots in the park and a popular place to spend the night. Across the bridge is the posted end of the Cross Trail and the Big Carp River Four-Bunk Cabin. Follow Lake Superior Trail west a short way and you will pass Lake Superior Cabin, a four-bunk unit, then come to the stairs that lead to the Big Carp River campsites.

Government Peak Trail

M-107 to North Mirror Lake Trail
Distances: 2 miles to Union Springs Trail
3.3 miles to Lost Lake Trail
5.2 miles to Government Peak
7.3 miles to North Mirror Lake Trail
Highest Point: 1,850 feet
Hiking Time: 5 to 7 hours

This is a 7.3-mile route that extends from a trailhead off M-107 then heads south to a junction with Lost Lake Trail and then west to merge into North Mirror Lake Trail, a mile from the popular lake. The first half, especially the area around Trap Falls, is very scenic and features backcountry campsites but no cabins or yurts.

The second half is a lightly traveled route where at times the brush is so thick during the summer that it obscures the path. This portion of the trail is not nearly as interesting, and while Government Peak may be the second highest point of the Porkies, the view at best is a very limited one from the top.

The trail, however, can be combined with North Mirror and the Escarpment trails to form a 16-mile loop with nights spent near Trap Falls and Mirror Lake. If you are contemplating this scenic trek, begin with Government Peak and follow North Mirror Lake Trail downhill to Lake of the Clouds, by far the easiest way to hike this trail.

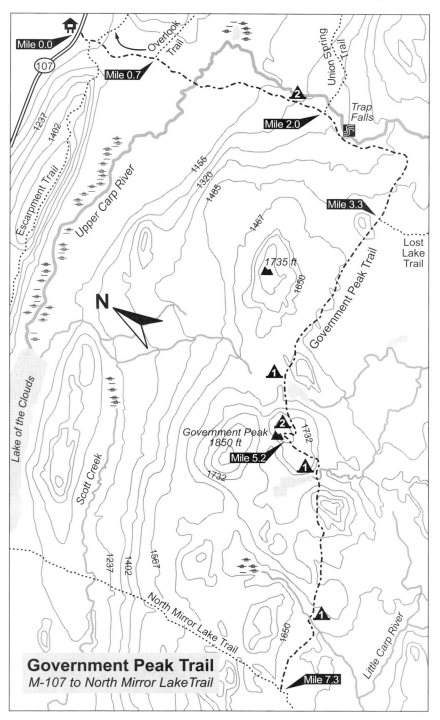

Mile 0.0

107

Overlook Trail

Mile 0.7

Union Spring Trail

2

Mile 2.0

Trap Falls

Mile 3.3

Lost Lake Trail

Escarpment Trail

Upper Carp River

1237

1402

1155

1320

1485

1467

1735 ft

1650

N

Government Peak Trail

Lake of the Clouds

Scott Creek

1

Government Peak
1850 ft

Mile 5.2

2

1732

1

1237

1402

1567

1732

North Mirror Lake Trail

1650

Little Carp River

1

Government Peak Trail
M-107 to North Mirror Lake Trail

Mile 7.3

M-107 to Lost Lake Trail

Distance: 3.3 miles

Government Peak Trail begins along M-107, 4 miles from the Escarpment Overlook. You begin with a steep climb to quickly pass the posted east end of the Escarpment Trail and then the first trailhead to the Overlook Trail. The trail levels out and then descends to the second trailhead of the Overlook, a 3-mile loop that climbs to 1,500 feet (See chapter 9). Here you find a huge trail sign that declares you have just hiked a mile from M-107. It is the fastest mile most backpackers have ever covered.

Government Peak continues south and crosses through a low-lying forest, a level but often wet and muddy stretch. Within a true mile from M-107, you cross Upper Carp River for the first time, a sluggish stream in a marshy area, but all this changes in a half mile. The trail cuts across the wide bend where the river swings west, and when it returns to the Upper Carp you are climbing through an old growth forest with a mountain stream gurgling alongside of you.

This very scenic gorge-like area is reached 1.5 miles from M-107, and located nearby are a pair of backcountry campsites with fire rings and a view of the river. You continue to climb into the gorge for the next half mile along a river that churns and swirls through an obstacle course of boulders, rocks, and ancient trees that have fallen across the water. The posted junction with Union Spring Trail is reached 2 miles from the M-107 trailhead. By heading east on this trail, you can reach the natural spring in 2 miles and South Boundary Road in 4 miles.

Government Peak continues climbing south and passes several scenic pools with the best one , Trap Falls, reached 0.4 mile from the junction. The cascade is well named as the Upper Carp tumbles 15 feet down a narrow rock ledge into a basin below that traps the river momentarily into a deep pool before letting it continue. A bench in a stand of towering pines completes this scenic spot but on a hot summer day you will find that many backpackers would rather sit in the pool than on the bench.

Government Peak Trail continues by climbing a small hill and then descends to the junction with Lost Lake Trail, 3.3 miles from

M-107. Lost Lake Trail leads to its namesake lake in 1.5 miles and South Boundary Road in 3.4 miles.

Lost Lake to North Mirror Lake Trail
Distance: 4 miles

At this point Government Peak swings west and begins its second half as a fairly level route. Within a mile the trail climbs a series of low ridges and crosses several small streams that are often dry during mid-summer. After the third stream, the trail levels out and 1.3 miles from the Lost Lake junction you break out at an open marsh with a large beaver pond in the middle. The pond is the headwaters for the Upper Carp and good place to sight a variety of wildlife including beavers, deer and waterfowl. There is a backcountry campsite nearby

Once you skirt the pond, the trail begins its ascent to Government Peak. It is a steady climb up and steep at times, but in a half mile you reach the peak where its elevation of 1,850 feet is posted near the stone foundations of a 1927 fire tower. The peak is reached 5.2 miles from M-107 and for most backpackers the view is anticlimactic. On the west side, however, it is possible to gaze through the trees into the interior of the park. There is a backcountry campsite near the peak and another on its west side.

Descending the peak to the west is at first a rapid downhill hike but overall not the steep slope experienced on the east side. Within a half mile you bottom out at a small creek that also feeds the Upper Carp River and nearby is a backcountry campsite. From there the trail is a level woods walk for the remaining 2 miles. This is where the trail can really be obscure and sometimes very muddy in places. Within 0.7 mile of North Mirror Lake Trail, you pass a backcountry campsite along a small stream and then the posted junction. The west end of Government Peak Trail is less than a mile from Mirror Lake and 2.9 miles from the Lake of the Clouds Overlook.

A backpacker crosses the Big Carp River at Lake of the Clouds along the North Mirror Lake Trail.

Chapter Eight

THE SHORT TRAILS

*Lost Lake • Correction Line • South and North
Mirror Lake • Pinkerton • Cross Trail*

Within the backcountry are a number of shorter trails that either serve as links between longer routes or provide access into the park from a road.

Correction Line Trail links Big Carp River with the trails at Mirror Lake while Cross Trail spans from Lake Superior Trail at the mouth of the Big Carp to Greenstone Falls. Pinkerton, Lost Lake and the Mirror Lake trails all provide access from South Boundary Road or, in the case of North Mirror Lake, from the Lake of the Clouds Overlook.

Dayhikers looking for possible routes should consider hiking into Lost Lake, a scenic stretch that makes for a round trip of 4 miles, or combine South Mirror Lake with a portion of Little Carp Trail, Beaver Creek Trail, and Summit Trail for a 5.5-mile loop that begins and ends at the top of Summit Peak Road.

Backpacker following a trail in the Porcupine Mountains backcountry.

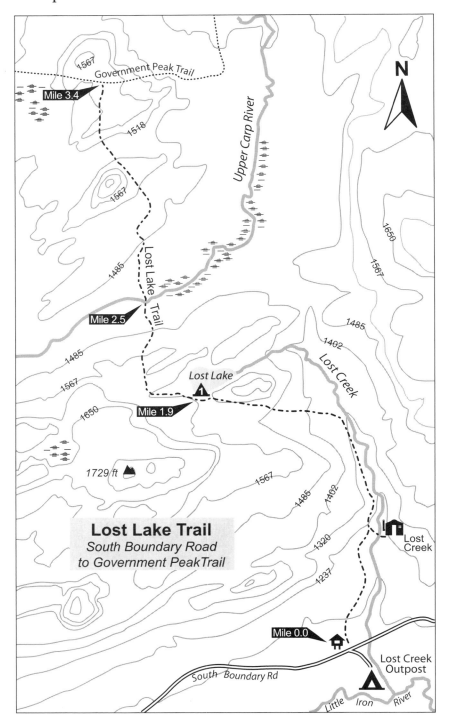

Lost Lake Trail

South Boundary Road to Government Peak Trail
    Distance: 1.9 miles to Lost Lake
              2.5 miles to Upper Carp River
              3.4 miles to Government Peak Trail
    Highest Point: 1,560 feet
    Hiking Time: 3 to 4 hours one-way

This trail extends from South Boundary Road to Government Peak Trail and along the way passes a yurt, a backcountry campsite, and, of course, its namesake lake, a small, remote, and beautiful body of water. There is considerable climbing and a steep descent on this route, but much of it is eliminated if you're only going to the lake itself, a moderately easy round-trip hike of 4 miles.

The trailhead is posted along South Boundary Road, 7 miles from M-107 and across from Lost Creek Outpost Campground where there is a hiker's parking area. The route begins as a level path through pines and hardwoods, appearing like the old mining road that it is. Within a half mile you arrive at a posted spur that leads east (right) across the stream to the Lost Creek Yurt on its east bank. The tent-like structure sleeps four and can be reserved in advance.

The trail/road then begins a gentle climb where it is carved into the side of a narrow ravine and soon puts you above Lost Creek with a scenic view of the water rushing below. Within a mile, the trail crosses a feeder creek. A few yards away there is a picturesque pool and a small cascade spilling into Lost Creek. At this point the trail departs the mining road and begins a steep ascent to the higher level of the lake. You climb for almost a mile until you top off at 1,560 feet in a virgin stand of hemlock and then emerge from the giant trees for your first view of the lake.

The small lake is really more like a very large pond with a shoreline guarded by a tangle of brush, an angler's nightmare if trying to cast from the edge. A belly boat would be excellent here though the lake is not stocked and few people bother to fish it. Waterfowl often gather at Lost Lake, and occasionally you can spot a deer feeding along the edge.

The trail skirts the south side of the lake, passing a backcountry campsite and arriving at a mileage sign at its southwest corner that informs you Government Peak Trail is still 2.5 miles away though the distance is more like 1.5 miles. From here the pines give way to a hardwood forest with thick underbrush, and the trail crosses the often wet west end of Lost Lake to begin a rapid descent. In the next half mile, you are gripping the straps of your backpack as the trail descends almost 160 feet off the ridge.

At 2.5 miles you bottom out at Upper Carp River. The headwaters for this river are ponds near Government Peak. From there the Upper Carp makes a loop to the south then north before eventually emptying into Lake of the Clouds. This is one of most scenic stretches of the river as well as one of the most remote. Anglers willing to bash some heavy brush might be rewarded with some excellent brook trout fishing by exploring downstream segments.

There is no bridge across Upper Carp, and although the river is considerably larger than Lost Creek, it is an easy ford during normal water levels. On the other side the trail climbs out of the Upper Carp valley in the final leg, but it is not nearly as steep as the south side. You gain only 80 feet before arriving at Government Peak Trail at a posted junction.

For those continuing on, Government Peak, the second highest point in the park, is 1.9 miles to the west and Mirror Lake lies 4.9 miles along Government Peak Trail. A pair of backcountry campsites are 1.8 miles north along the same trail, and M-107 is 3.3 miles. To the west along Government Peak Trail are five backcountry campsites.

Correction Line Trail

Big Carp River to Mirror Lake
   Distance: 2.8 miles
   Highest Point: 1,600 feet
   Hiking Time: 1.5 to 2 hours
Correction Line Trail is a well traveled route that connects Big Carp River Trail, 4 miles from Lake Superior or 5 miles from the Lake of the Clouds Overlook, to Mirror Lake. It's commonly used to form a loop from Lake Superior to Mirror Lake and back to M-107. By combining portions of Lake Superior Trail and Big

Carp River and returning on Correction Line and North Mirror Lake Trail, backpackers can undertake a 21-mile, three to four-day trip through some of the most scenic sections of the Porkies.

Named for the "correction line" cartographers use to adjust flat maps to the earth's curvature, the trail departs from a junction reached just after the Big Carp River Trail crosses to south side of the river. The first part lies in a low-lying forest that is notorious for being muddy even in fair weather. After a heavy rain, the mud can suck your boots right off your feet.

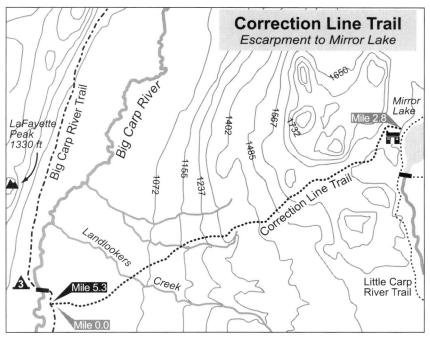

Within 0.7 mile you cross Landlookers Creek. Landlookers were timber cruisers hired by the lumber companies in the 19th century to search and map out stands of pine. Ironically, this is one section the lumber barons never touched as much of Correction Line passes through virgin stands of hemlock as well as impressive tracts of maples and yellow birch. Once across the creek, the trail begins its long climb to the higher level of the lake.

You climb 200 feet in the next half mile where the trail crosses a small creek and crosses to the other side of a ravine. Then you begin climbing again, this time along a much steeper section as

Correction Line takes you quickly from 1,300 to 1,584 feet. You top off on the edge of Big Carp River drainage and, in the fall, views of the valley below are possible.

The trail levels out when it enters a small hollow of old growth timber enclosed to the north by impressive rock bluffs. The only thing more impressive is the mud. It gets deeper still. The natural inclination is to hike around the mud holes, but that only makes the situation worse for others. It is really best to hike right through the mud and wash your boots at the end of the day.

The final half mile begins with a climb over a 1,600-foot knob and ends with the lake coming into view for the first time. A rapid descent puts you at Mirror Lake's north shoreline and a posted junction where the trail ends. Lake Superior is 11.8 miles to the west via the Little Carp River Trail, and departing east here is North Mirror Lake Trail, which reaches the Lake of the Clouds Overlook in 4 miles. Follow Little Carp River Trail to pass the Two-Bunk Cabin and then the South Mirror Lake Trail to reach four backcountry campsites. Head east to check out the other cabins and other campsites.

The Mirror Lake Eight-Bunk Cabin.

North & South Mirror Lake Trails

South Boundary Road to Escarpment Overlook
    Distance: 3 miles to Mirror Lake (via South Trail)
              7.3 miles to Escarpment Overlook
    Highest Point: 1,760 feet
    Hiking Time: 4 to 5 hours

The North and South Mirror Lake Trails provide a route that crosses the heart of the Porkies, beginning from Summit Peak Road and ending at the Lake of the Clouds Overlook. The highest point is quickly reached along the southern portion, but the northern half features the most climbing, especially if you are hiking into the lake from the Escarpment.

The South Trail is the shortest and easiest route to popular Mirror Lake with its three cabins and seven backcountry campsites, a trek of 3 miles. North Mirror Lake Trail is often used as a return to the M-107 for backpackers who begin on the Lake Superior Trail. For that reason, it will be described from south to north, by far the easiest way to hike this rugged route.

Mirror Lake with the rowboats from the cabins.

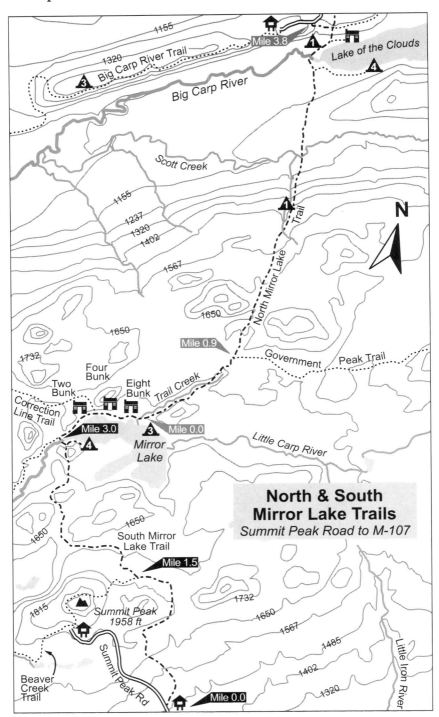

1155

1320

Big Carp River Trail

3

Mile 3.8

1

Lake of the Clouds

4

Big Carp River

Scott Creek

1155

1237

1320

1402

1567

1650

N

North Mirror Lake Trail

1

1732

1650

Mile 0.9

Government   Peak Trail

Four
Bunk

Two
Bunk

Eight
Bunk

Trail Creek

Correction
Line Trail

Mile 3.0

4

Mile 0.0

3

Little Carp River

Mirror
Lake

**North & South
Mirror Lake Trails**

Summit Peak Road to M-107

1650

1650

South Mirror
Lake Trail

Mile 1.5

1732

1815

Summit Peak
1958 ft

1650

1567

1485

Little Iron River

Beaver
Creek
Trail

Summit Peak Rd

Mile 0.0

1402

1320

South Mirror Trail

Distance: 3 miles to Mirror Lake

A trailhead with limited parking is located 1.5 miles up Summit Peak Road. If the parking area is full, a larger one for overflow is located at the beginning of the road. The trail departs north from here as a forest road that is used off-season by the staff as a service drive into the heart of the park.

You climb more than 200 feet from your car or the trailhead, topping off at 1,760 feet in the first half mile. At this point the trail begins to skirt Summit Peak. At 1,958 feet, Summit Peak is the highest point in the park and third highest in the state. Eventually the trail descends the ridge and quickly arrives at a posted junction with the Summit Peak Trail, 1.5 miles from the trailhead. The view from the peak is nice, but it is a steep, 258-foot climb to the top from here.

South Mirror Lake Trail continues north as a forest road descending gently until it bottoms out at small stream and becomes a true foot path 2.1 miles into the hike. On the other side it climbs to 1,640 feet, crosses a ridge, and then descends to the Little Carp River. Just before crossing the river, you pass the spur that leads to four backcountry campsites located on a long inlet that forms the west end of the lake.

On the other side is the posted junction with Little Carp River Trail. From here Lily Pond is 2.8 miles to the west and the three cabins on the north side are a short walk to the east. At 1,532 feet, Mirror Lake is the highest lake in the park and one of the highest in the state. It is surrounded by rugged bluffs and ridges, many which can be climbed for views of the area, while towering pines dominate much of the shoreline. The trail skirts the lake first passing a spur to the Two-Bunk Cabin and later a posted junction to Correction Line Trail.

Just beyond the junction is the Four-Bunk Cabin located near the lake in a stand of towering pine. Finally, you reach the Eight-Bunk Cabin, a virtual log lodge perched right above the water. You need to continue along the trail past the large cabin to pick up the North Mirror Lake Trail or reach three more backcountry campsites along the east side of the lake.

North Mirror Lake Trail
  Distances: *0.9 mile to Government Peak Trail*
         3.3 miles to Lake of the Clouds
         3.8 miles to Escarpment

North Mirror Lake Trail extends from the lake to the Lake of the Clouds Overlook, a 3.8-mile trek that takes most hikers almost three hours to walk. From the shoreline, the North Mirror Lake quickly crosses a creek and then parallels Trail Creek as it climbs a low ridge. This section is often wet and muddy from heavy use even though you are well above the creek. Within a mile you come to the posted junction with the Government Peak Trail.

Government Peak heads east to reach the 1850-foot high point in 2.1 miles. North Mirror Lake Trail departs the junction to the north and begins a gentle ascent while in a mile you top off at 1640 feet. This stretch can also be muddy at times but scenic in October when the fallen leaves give way to views of 1700-foot ridges on both sides of you. Nearby is a backcountry campsite.

Beyond the ridges, the trail begins a long descent, easy walking at first, but 2 miles from the lake the trek becomes a knee-bending drop. If coming from the Lake of the Clouds Overlook, you will find this is one of the steepest climbs in the park. In 0.75 mile, you descend from 1,640 feet to 1,160 through a gorge-like area where a tributary of Scott Creek rushes downhill. Keep your eyes peeled for trail blazes in the trees as it's easy to get turned around here.

You bottom out to cross Scott Creek, climb over a 1,200-foot ridge and at 3.3 miles from the lake arrive at the west end of Lake of the Clouds. A spur heads left to a series of four backcountry campsites. A long boardwalk crosses a stream emptying into the lake here and makes for a unique viewing point. You cannot see much of the famous lake, but you can look above to spot people staring down at you from the Lake of the Clouds Overlook.

The trail swings to the east, passes a backcountry campsite along the shoreline of the lake, and then comes to the spur that leads to the Lake of Clouds Cabin a quarter mile away. The final half mile is a steep march uphill as the trail becomes a series of switchbacks, gaining more than 150 feet from the level of the lake until finally breaking out at the M-107 parking lot at 1,246 feet. Along the way you pass a posted junction to the west end of the Escarpment Trail.

Lake of the Clouds, one of the most photographed lakes in the state.

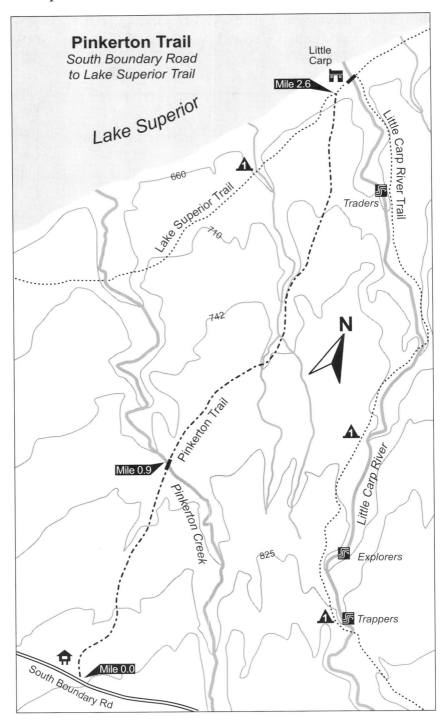

Pinkerton Trail
*South Boundary Road
to Lake Superior Trail*

Lake Superior

Little Carp

Mile 2.6

Little Carp River Trail

660

Lake Superior Trail

710

Traders

742

N

Pinkerton Trail

Mile 0.9

Little Carp River

Pinkerton Creek

825

Explorers

Trappers

Mile 0.0

South Boundary Rd

Pinkerton Trail

South Boundary Road to Little Carp River Trail
Distance: 2.6 miles
Highest Point: 1,060 feet
Hiking Time: 1 to 2 hours

Pinkerton Trail is the shortest route to the cabins and campsites near the mouth of the Big Carp River, a popular destination for many hikers. The trail itself is 2.6 miles, making the journey to the Big Carp a one-way trek of roughly 4 miles. Pinkerton is also a scenic walk, passing through impressive stands of virgin hemlock and crossing several bridged streams and creeks along the way.

The trailhead is posted along South Boundary Road, 5 miles east of Presque Isle and 20 miles west from the Visitor's Center. There is limited parking here.

From the trailhead you quickly enter the old growth forest, a stand of impressive hemlocks and later northern hardwoods such as maple and yellow birch. The trail begins with a mild descent through the forest and in less than a mile arrives at the Pinkerton Creek bridge. On the other side you climb the bank, level out briefly, then descend to cross a feeder creek on a slab bridge.

The trail levels out after this, angling towards Little Carp River through the impressive forest and at one point passes a lighting-struck tree posted with "1988," the year of the storm. Within 1.2 miles of crossing Pinkerton, you emerge on the edge of the Little Carp River Gorge to see the rushing stream below. From here it is a gradual half mile descent to the Lake Superior Trail junction.

To the west, Presque Isle River is a 6.3-mile trek while Little Carp River Cabin is just up the trail to the east. The mouth of the Big Carp River is still 1.3 miles to the east but reached along a very scenic stretch of the Lake Superior Trail that hugs the shoreline.

Cross Trail

Lake Superior to Greenstone Falls
   Map on page 67
   Distance: 4.5 miles to Little Carp River Trail
   Highest Point: 1,220 feet
   Hiking Time: 3 to 4 hours

Cross Trail is probably the least traveled route in the park. It connects the Lake Superior Trail at the mouth of the Big Carp River with the Little Carp River Trail near Greenstone Falls. It is a 4.5-mile trek, but most backpackers choose to follow Little Carp River instead, a longer hike (7.3 miles to the Greenstone Falls) but a much more scenic route. Or if they are entering the park, they reach the Big Carp River via Pinkerton and Lake Superior Trails, a 4-mile walk.

Cross Trail is level for the most part but can be wet, especially in the middle when it crosses Memengwa Swamp, and at times is hard to follow. Since there are usually few people on the trail, chances of spotting wildlife are excellent. In most places there will be far more deer tracks in the mud than foot prints, and it is rare to hike this trail without seeing at least one set of bear prints.

From the west bank of the Big Carp River, the trail is posted at its junction with the Lake Superior Trail and immediately passes the four-bunk cabin. The trail stays near the river for the next half mile, winding along a series of interesting pools until you reach Bathtub Falls. At one time this was the start of the Big Carp River Trail and a set of orange blazes still marks where you would have crossed the river.

At this point Cross Trail swings away from the water and makes its steepest climb of the day. You ascend more than 80 feet to the top of a bluff and are rewarded with a fine view of the Big Carp flowing through a series of rapids far below. You follow the river briefly, then the trail swings away from the Big Carp for good, and in a half mile you descend to cross a feeder creek.

Cross Trail then turns into a woods walk through an old growth forest for the next mile and is level with the exception of crossing three streams. The third is Toledo Creek that flows through a small ravine. You remain in the forest for another half mile and then enter the wet section of the route, 2.5 miles from Lake Superior.

This is sloppy hiking with mud burying your boots even during a dry spell. It will also be "buggy," but there is one plus. Wildlife tracks will be all around you. The half-pear prints of whitetail deer will be the most common tracks seen, but look around, if the deer flies will allow it, and there's a good chance you will spot bear prints. Bear tracks look more like a human foot than they do dog tracks, but they have a larger, more rounded pad and often the claws are clearly visible. Those more than four inches wide indicate a good size bruin has passed through.

Within a half mile the wet low-lying woods turns into a grassy marsh-like opening before Cross Trail returns to the woods. In all, it is roughly a mile of hard slogging before you leave the swamp behind and enter the final portion of the trail, a very gradual ascent through a pleasant stand hemlock to the high point of 1,220 feet. From here you drop quickly to the Little Carp Trail junction.

At this point Section 17 Cabin lies just across the river. Greenstone Falls Cabin is a quarter mile west along Little Carp River Trail and Mirror Lake is 5.8 miles.

A day hiker carefully crosses a marshy area along the Cross Trail.

A pair hikers tackle a climb along the Escarpment Trail.

Chapter Nine

DAYHIKES

Escarpment Trail • Overlook Trail • Whitetail Path • Visitor Center Nature Trail • Union Mine Trail • Union Spring Trail • Summit Peak Trail • Beaver Creek and Lily Pond Trails • Greenstone Falls Access Trail • East and West River Trails

---

Need to stretch your legs? Have a spare hour in the park or an afternoon? Or are some of your hiking partners too young to tackle the 16-mile-long Lake Superior Trail? Porcupine Mountains may be a wilderness but it's also a state park with a wide variety of hiking opportunities. Many trails around its perimeter make for excellent dayhikes.

The best, by far, is the 4-mile-long Escarpment Trail, perhaps the most scenic hike in the Midwest. Others are scenic loops, including East/West River Trails, Overlook Trail, and Summit Peak Trail when combined with a portion of South Mirror Lake Trail.

If young children are a part of your hiking party, try the Union Mine Trail, the Access Trail to Greenstone Falls, or the East/West River Trails. All three treks are 2 miles or shorter in length and can be handled by most children as young as four or five years old.

Perhaps the most popular short hike in the park is the descent from the Escarpment along North Mirror Lake Trail to the bridge across Big Carp River and then the steep climb back up, a round trip of 1.5 miles. The start of other long trails that make for scenic dayhikes include the first 2 miles of Big Carp River Trail (See page 74) and the beginning of the Lake Superior Trail from M-107 (See page 54).

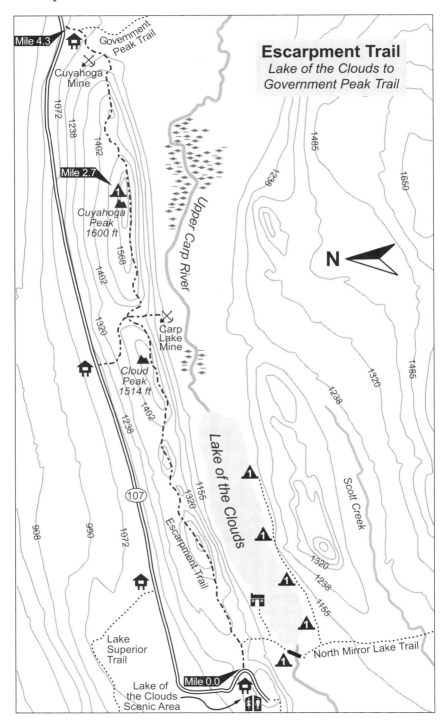

Escarpment Trail
*Lake of the Clouds to
Government Peak Trail*

Mile 4.3

Government
Peak Trail

Cuyahoga
Mine

1072

1238

1402

Mile 2.7

Cuyahoga
Peak
1600 ft

1568

Upper Carp River

1485

1238

1650

N

1402

1320

Carp
Lake
Mine

Cloud
Peak
1514 ft

1402

1238

1320

1238

107

Escarpment Trail

1155

1320

Lake of the Clouds

Scott Creek

1320

1238

908

990

1072

1155

North Mirror Lake Trail

Lake
Superior
Trail

Mile 0.0

Lake of
the Clouds
Scenic Area

Escarpment Trail

Lake of the Clouds to Government Peak Trail
  Distance: 4.3 miles
  Highest Point: 1,600 feet
  Hiking Time: 2 to 3 hours

This is the crowning jewel of trails not only in the Porkies but in all of Michigan and possibly in the Midwest. The Escarpment combines a high rocky bluff and alpine-like vistas with views of the park's rugged interior, Big Carp River Valley, and, of course, the centerpiece of the park, Lake of Clouds. Unlike the tourists who simply drive to the overlook and look down, the Escarpment Trail provides you with views of the famous lake from several different angles, and if the day is clear, you can easily fill your memory card with stunning digital images by the time you return to M-107.

The only drawback is that the Escarpment is a point-to-point trail. You begin here; you end up over there, 4.3 miles from your vehicle. There is a spur reached halfway along the trail that can be used to access M-107 after 2 miles, and, of course, you can always turn around and simply retrace your steps. However, it would be a shame to go that far to hike one of the most awe-inspiring trails in the Midwest and not finish it.

The easiest direction to follow the route is beginning from the Lake of the Clouds Overlook. Before departing remember to fill the water bottles. There is no drinking water at the overlook, and on a clear summer day the route across the Escarpment can be a hot one. You actually begin at the posted North Mirror Lake Trailhead and for a half mile the trail dips and climbs along the Escarpment as a rock and boulder-strewn path.

At a well-posted junction, North Mirror Lake Trail plummets towards Lake of the Clouds while the Escarpment officially begins with a climb through a mixed forest of pines and young oaks. Quickly you arrive at the first overlook, staring down at the middle of the lake. The trail resumes with a sharper climb, and in a half mile you break out at a second vista. This vista is spectacular, as good or better than the overlook at the end of M-107 because you're much higher at 1,480. At your feet, 400 feet straight down, is Lake of the Clouds in royal blue. To the west you can see visitors who have just stepped out of their cars and to the east is the rest of the Escarpment and the Upper Carp River winding its way into the lake.

The trail continues along the open cliff for a few hundred yards where you enjoy the scenery every step of the way before dipping into the woods. You cross two small knobs, one with a view, make a rapid descent, and then begin the climb to Cloud Peak. The trail skirts the 1,514-foot high point, and for the first time in the hike you are standing at the east end of the lake and viewing it in its entirety to the west along with the rocky bluff. It is even possible to see a portion of Government Peak on the horizon to the south.

At one time this spectacular view was the only view for most people. Before the Porkies became a state park in 1945, M-107 ended 2 miles short of where it does today, and visitors were faced with a half mile trek to Cloud Peak to see Lake of the Clouds.

From Cloud Peak, the trail makes another rapid descent and reaches the junction with the Cutoff Trail 2.3 miles from the overlook. The spur heads north (left) to descend to M-107 in less than a half mile and can be used to turn the first half of the Escarpment Trail into a 4-mile loop with a return along the park road. Why anyone would want to return along a paved road with vehicle traffic instead of simply backtracking a foot trail along the Escarpment is beyond me.

To the south (right) is a trail to the site of Carp Lake Mine, a short side trip to see the twin boilers and other remains of the stamping mill. Carp Lake was the name for Lake of the Clouds when the mine was established in 1858. The operation lingered into the 1920s but reached its peak in 1865 when a company of more than 50 men used a small stamping mill to produce 13,000 pounds of copper from several shafts into the Escarpment.

The Escarpment Trail continues straight and immediately begins its ascent to Cuyahoga Peak. You climb more than 200 feet to close in on the 1,600-foot peak and in less than a half mile from the junction you arrive at another panoramic vista, this one centering on the Upper Carp River. Here the trail hugs the edge of the Escarpment while skirting the wooded top of Cuyahoga Peak. A bit farther, reached 2.7 miles from the overlook parking area is the Cuyahoga Peak backcountry campsite.

The site is posted and features only a fire ring and enough flat space for one maybe two small tents, but its location is amazing. It's set back slightly in the trees, yet three steps away is the edge of the rocky bluff where you can sit all night and watch the stars or possibly the Northern Lights reflect off Lake of the Clouds. Return in the morning and you can watch another day begin.

The trail continues by beginning its long descent off the Escarpment. You quickly pass the only view of Lake Superior and then begin a steep portion of the descent. The trail levels out briefly to pass Cuyahoga Mine posted with the year "1856." The mine never produced a profitable amount of copper and probably died out in 1866 when Carp Lake mine was first shut down. All that remains today is a long open ditch-like digging.

The mine is only a quarter mile from the trail's east end, but it is a steep quarter mile and you're practically running downhill when you arrive at the junction with Government Peak. Head north to reach M-107 in a quarter mile and south to stay in the interior of the park along Government Peak Trail.

A hiker along the Escarpment Trail,
looking at the Upper Carp River.

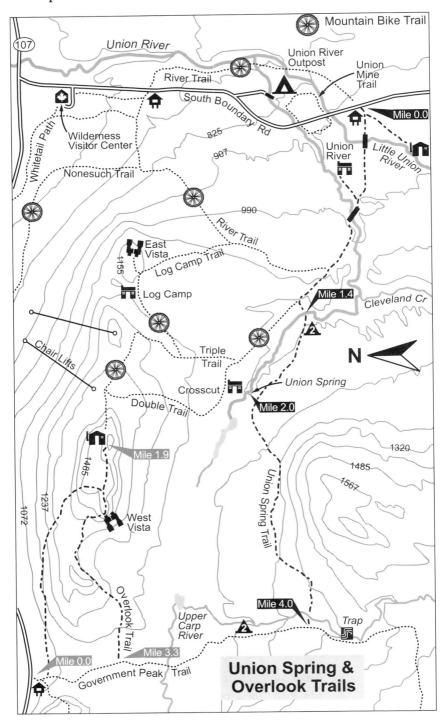

Mountain Bike Trail

Union River

107

Union River
Outpost

Union
Mine
Trail

River Trail

South Boundary Rd

Mile 0.0

Whitetail Path

Wilderness
Visitor Center

825

Union
River

Little Union
River

907

Nonesuch Trail

990

River Trail

East
Vista

Log Camp Trail

1155

Log Camp

Cleveland Cr

Mile 1.4

Chair Lifts

Triple
Trail

Union Spring

N

Crosscut

Double Trail

Mile 2.0

1320

1485

Mile 1.9

1485

1567

1237

West
Vista

1072

Union Spring Trail

Overlook Trail

Mile 4.0

Trap

Upper
Carp
River

Mile 0.0

Mile 3.3

Government Peak Trail

Union Spring & Overlook Trails

Overlook Trail

Round Trip from M-107

    Distance: 4 miles
    Highest Point: 1,510 feet
    Hiking Time: 2 to 4 hours

The Overlook Trail offers one of the few loops into the rugged interior of the park that is under 10 miles in length, making it an ideal day hike for those with only a few hours left on their itinerary. The trail begins and ends off M-107, climbs to 1,500 feet and passes two viewing areas that provide a glimpse into the heart of the Porkies. All this on a hike that's only 3 miles long. Add a sleeping bag to your pack, another mile to your hike, and a little advance planning to your trip, and you can spend the night on top of the ridge at the West Vista Yurt. Don't be misled by the short distances, however. This is still a challenging trek with long steep climbs and poor footings in many places.

You pick up the Overlook at the Government Peak Trailhead, posted along M-107 3.5 miles west of South Boundary Road. You actually begin and end on Government Peak Trail but only briefly. The wide trail quickly climbs to its junction with the Escarpment Trail then intersects with the north end of the Overlook, a junction that can be easily missed by those not looking for it.

The Overlook begins by descending to a small stream, climbing out of the gully, and then passing through a wet area for the next 0.3 mile. This ends when the trail enters a stand of stately virgin hemlock. The trees are stunning, especially when most people have to lean back to see the tops. At this point keep a sharp eye out for trail blazes on the trunks as the trail is not well defined in places.

A half mile into the hike, the Overlook begins a steady climb, levels out briefly among the towering pines, and climbs again. The second ascent is a steep one for more than a quarter mile before you top out in a forest of hardwoods at 1,510 feet. Here the foot path merges with a two-track that is a ski trail during the winter and open to mountain bikers the rest of the year. Head east (left) on the ski/bike trail and within 0.3 mile you arrive at the West Vista Yurt. The octagonal tent is pitched on the crest of the ridge at an elevation of almost 1,500 feet. Needless to say it's a most unusual place to spend a night.

From the junction with the ski/bike trail, the first view is only a short descent away, and you reach it 2.2 miles into the hike (including hiking to the West Vista Yurt, 1.6 miles if you skip it). Referred to as the West Vista, the high point is far better in September when leaves have fallen and the rest are changing color. In the winter, it is the highlight for many cross country skiers as they can look down the Carp River Valley, past Lake of the Clouds and the Escarpment all the way to Lake Superior.

From this overlook, the trail loses much of the elevation you have just worked so hard to gain in a rapid drop of 140 feet through mostly virgin pines. At 2.8 miles you come to the second viewing point of the park's interior. The view depends on the season. In mid-summer, you have to stand on your toes to get a glimpse south of the park's rugged interior.

The trail continues with another sharp descent of 180 feet and at 3 miles levels out in a stand of pines. Keep an eye out for tree blazes here as they will lead through the pines for the next 0.3 mile to a well-posted junction with Government Peak Trail. Although the sign says it is a mile to M-107, it's actually much closer to 0.7 mile. The trail crosses a wet area that is well planked and then climbs slightly as a wide, unmistakable path. You finish off the day with a descent to M-107, passing the earlier junctions to the Escarpment and Overlook.

Whitetail Path

Union Bay Campground to the Visitor Center
Distance: 0.8 mile
Highest Point: 660 feet
Hiking Time: 30 minutes

Whitetail Path begins on the south side of M-107 near Union Bay Campground and parallels the state road before swinging south to emerge at the parking lot of the Visitor's Center. The trail is used primarily by campers to reach the interpretive center or park headquarters.

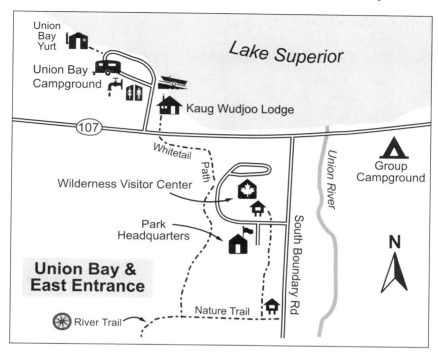

Visitor Center Nature Trail

Round Trip From Visitor Center
   Distance: 1.4 mile
   Highest Point: 700 feet
   Hiking Time: 30 to 45 minutes

Just off the entrance of the Visitor Center is the start of this nature trail, a 1.4 mile-long loop with a series of interpretive plaques along it. The trail heads south, passes the park headquarters, and then briefly merges into River Trail, an old logging road that is also part of the cross country ski/mountain bike trail network. Eventually you come to a junction with the Whitetail Path just before arriving at the Visitor Center parking lot.

Union Mine Trail

Round Trip from South Boundary Road
Distance: 1 mile
Highest Point: 880 feet
Hiking Time: 30 to 45 minutes

Union Mine Trail is the other interpretive trail in the park and features 17 numbered posts that correspond to an informative brochure. The brochure is available at the Visitor's Center or during the summer at the trailhead parking lot, reached 1.7 miles south of M-107 on South Boundary Road.

The trail is posted on the north side of the parking lot and hiked in clockwise direction by first heading towards Union River. You immediately reach the site of Union Mine where post number one marks the oldest copper operation in the Porkies, dating back to 1845 when the first shaft was sunk.

At Union River, the trail descends downstream, crosses South Boundary Road, and just before reaching Union River Outpost Campground cuts across to Little Union River. At either of the rivers it is possible to leave the trail and continue downstream to view a number of small cascades that form during the spring or after heavy rainfalls. The last leg of the trail is to follow Little Union River upstream back across South Boundary Road to the parking lot. The trail overall is easy, but this stretch involves climbing about 100 feet.

Union Spring Trail

South Boundary Road to Government Peak Trail
Distance: 4 miles
Highest Point: 1,300 feet
Hiking Time: 2 to 3 hours

Technically, Union Spring Trail is an access route into the park's interior and not a day hike as it extends 4 miles from South Boundary Road to Government Peak Trail. Along the way it passes the second largest natural spring in Michigan, and that's the reason most visitors walk the trail. A trek just to the spring and back makes for an enjoyable and easy 4-mile hike highlighted by the crystal clear pool of Union Spring.

The trail also passes a pair of backcountry campsites near an impoundment. These sites are an ideal designation for a family interested in an overnight trip to ease young children into backpacking. Children as young as 5 years old can easily handle the 1.5-mile level walk to the backcountry sites.

The trailhead for Union Spring is on South Boundary Road 2 miles south of M-107, just beyond the posted Union Mine Trail. The walk begins on an old logging road that quickly crosses Little Union River and in a half mile comes to a locked gate. Beyond the gate, the forest closes in as the trail crosses Union River and then makes a short ascent, the only climb on the way to the spring.

You pass the posted spur to Union River Cabin and within a mile from the trailhead come to a junction. The trail heads west at this point. Continuing in a northwest direction is an old logging road that is groomed in the winter for cross country skiers and is used by mountain bikers the rest of the year. From the junction the Union Spring Impoundment is quickly reached and nearby are the backcountry campsites, consisting of two tent pads and fire rings.

The spring itself is another half mile along a level route through old growth hardwoods and hemlock. The route can be wet at times, but the surrounding forest is impressive. Union Spring appears as small pond with a viewing platform extending out to the middle of it. From the end of the platform, you can gaze into the deep but clear pool to see the spring bubbling out of the ground at more than 700 gallons a minute.

The spring marks the halfway point to Government Peak Trail, and the remaining 2 miles begin in a low-lying, marshy area... a good place to spot wildlife—a bad place to be without bug dope. Within a mile of the spring, the trail curves to the south and begins a steady ascent of more than 100 feet. You actually top off at 1,300 feet and from there descend quickly into the Upper Carp River Gorge. At the river itself, an easy ford puts you on the west bank at the junction with Government Peak Trail. Head north along this trail to reach a pair of scenic backcountry campsites in a quarter mile and M-107 in 2 miles. Head south to reach Trap Falls in less than a half mile.

Summit Peak Tower Trail

Summit Peak Road to South Mirror Lake Trail
> *Distance: 0.5 mile to Summit Peak Tower*
>   *1 mile to South Mirror Lake Trail*
> *Highest Point: 1,958 feet*
> *Hiking Time: 1 hour*

From the picnic area and parking lot at the end of Summit Peak Road, a wide trail makes a steady ascent towards the park's highest peak. Planking and long staircases assist you in climbing the 258 feet to the tower, but it's still a steady climb, especially for older visitors and young children.

Within 0.4 mile you arrive at a viewing platform with benches. From the deck you are rewarded with a good view of the park's rugged interior including the marshes that the Little Carp River passes through. The trail continues to climb, and shortly you arrive at the 40-foot high, 60-step tower at the top of Summit Peak, third highest point in Michigan at 1,958 feet.

It is debatable how extensive the view from the tower is, but on a clear day some claim to view the ski flying ramp on top of Copper Peak to the northwest. Most visitors have a hard time spotting Lake Superior and the small bit of Mirror Lake's shoreline much less Wisconsin or the Apostle Islands. The view is still impressive, however, as the ruggedness of the Porkies is as evident here as any overlook in the park.

The second half of the trail is a straight drop off the peak, with some sections being extremely steep. Caution should be used and the switchbacks followed as you descend a half mile from the peak to South Mirror Lake Trail, 1.5 miles from the lake itself. By heading south (right) at the junction, you could turn the outing into a 3-mile loop by following South Mirror Lake Trail as it gently descends a mile to Summit Peak Road. The loop would be completed by hiking up the road to your vehicle.

Crossing a boardwalk along the Beaver Creek Trail

Beaver Creek and Lily Pond Trails

Round Trip from Summit Peak Road
>*Distance: 5 miles*
>*Highest Point: 1,700 feet*
>*Hiking Time: 3 to 4 hours*

These two trails plus a portion of Little Carp River Trail form a pleasant half-day hike along a route that is scenic but not nearly as heavily traveled during the summer as the Escarpment or the Mirror Lake Trails. Throw in the mile that people with only one vehicle have to hike along Summit Peak Road from one trailhead to other and this outing is a 6-mile day.

It is an easier hike if you start with Beaver Creek Trail at the parking area at the end of Summit Peak Road. Keep in mind, however, parking is very limited here and the lot is often filled on a clear day. If that's the case, consider parking at the Lily Pond Trailhead and beginning with the park road.

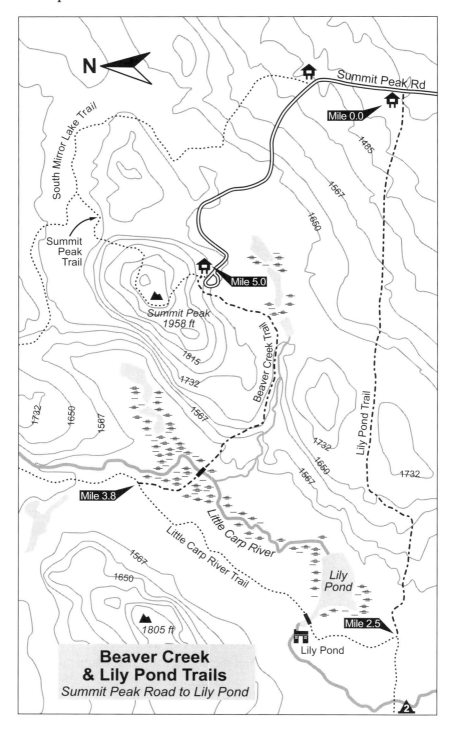

N

South Mirror Lake Trail

Summit Peak Rd

Mile 0.0

1485

1567

1650

Summit
Peak
Trail

Mile 5.0

Summit Peak
1958 ft

Beaver Creek Trail

Lily Pond Trail

1815

1732

1732

1650

1567

1732

1567

1650

1732

Mile 3.8

Little Carp River

Little Carp River Trail

1567

1650

1805 ft

Lily
Pond

Mile 2.5

Lily Pond

**Beaver Creek
& Lily Pond Trails**
Summit Peak Road to Lily Pond

2

Beaver Creek Trail

Distance: 2 miles to Lily Pond

Beaver Creek begins near the toilet building, wanders into the maple forest and immediately arrives at second trailhead posted where the foot path swings away from an old logging road. The trail is clearly marked and from here crosses a small stream and then makes rapid descent from the Summit Peak area into a gorge formed by the so called Beaver Creek, though it is not labeled on maps. This downhill walk is an impressive stretch as you follow the stream through the steep-sided and boulder-strewn gorge.

Eventually you bottom out and swing away from the creek to pass the old logging road once again and arrive at the extensive marsh area surrounding Little Carp River. A bridge and then planking with a small knob of dry ground in the middle provides dry footing across the marsh to the junction of Little Carp River Trail on the other side. Take your time crossing for the opportunities to sight wildlife, including beavers, are very good here.

At the posted junction, Mirror Lake is 1.5 miles north (right) along Little Carp River Trail while Lily Pond is 0.8 mile to the south (left). Heading south, the trail is a level walk through a mix of hardwoods and pines with an occasional wet area to step through before you break out at the impressive bridge across Little Carp River. The huge wooden structure features a bench in the middle angled towards the view of Lily Pond and the surrounding ridges. The bench and the view make the bridge a great place for an extended break or lunch.

Lily Pond Trail

Distance: 3 miles

Little Carp River Trail departs into an impressive stand of white pine and in less than a half mile reaches the posted junction with Lily Pond Trail. Continue with the Little Carp River Trail and you will reach Lake Superior in 9 miles.

Head east on Lily Pond Trail to return to Summit Peak Road in 2.5 miles. You immediately pass a pair of old tree stump chairs that have been cleverly carved with a chainsaw and now are padded with green moss. Who says park rangers aren't creative? Shortly beyond them the trail begins its ascent out of the Little Carp River valley.

The climb is gentle and along the way you move from pines into a virgin stand of maple and beech and pass some impressively large trunks. Thimbleberry patches will also begin appearing, and if your timing is right you will be stopping at every splash of red along the trail. There is one steep but short pitch a mile from Little Carp River Trail that ends with the high point of 1,720 feet where a bench has been built.

Once over the top, the trail makes a steady descent for a half mile to cross a stream at 1,500 feet and enters a towering stand of hemlock. The mile-long descent to Summit Park Road at 1,400 feet is much more gentle and you will cross one last stream just before breaking out at the parking lot.

Thimbleberry plant with a berry

Greenstone Falls Access Trail

Little Carp Road to Greenstone Falls
  Map on page 70
  Distance: 0.75 miles
  Highest Point: 1,300 feet
  Hiking Time: 30 minutes

This trail is used by many to gain quick access to both Section 17 and Greenstone Falls cabins but also makes for an easy round-trip day hike of 1.5 miles past several cascades. The trailhead is posted at the end of Little Carp River Road, reached 9 miles from Presque Isle or 16 miles from the Visitor Center.

The trail departs along the river bank and within 100 feet comes to Overlooked Falls, a pair of cascades with a total drop of 10 feet. The second one is quite scenic as it is split in the middle by a huge boulder. The trail stays briefly on top of the small gorge the Little Carp River cuts here and then descends into it via a set of steps.

At the bottom you cross the river at a massive log jam where one huge pine has been cut into a foot bridge. The trail climbs out of the gorge on the other side to the junction with the Little Carp River Trail. Greenstone Falls is a mere 100 yards west along the Little Carp and is a scenic spot. Set in a small gorge, the cascade features a 15-foot wide veil that tumbles down a series of rock steps and small boulders. Continue west along Little Carp River Trail to reach Greenstone Falls Cabin in another 100 yards and Section 17 Cabin in less than a half mile.

117

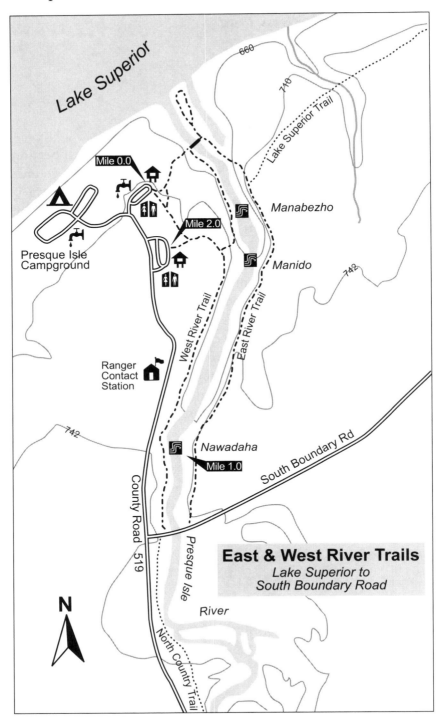

Lake Superior

660

740

Lake Superior Trail

Mile 0.0

Manabezho

Mile 2.0

Manido

742

Presque Isle
Campground

West River Trail

East River Trail

Ranger
Contact
Station

742

Nawadaha

Mile 1.0

South Boundary Rd

East & West River Trails
*Lake Superior to
South Boundary Road*

County Road 519

Presque Isle

River

N

North Country Trail

East and West River Trails

Round Trip from Presque Isle Day-use Area
    Distance: 2 miles
    Highest Point: 700 feet
    Hiking Time: 1 hour

The East River Trail and the West River Trail are actually two separate paths, but when combined, as they usually are, they form another scenic loop in the Porkies and the best trek for families with young children. The outing packs in adventure, stands of virgin hemlock, waterfalls, and great scenery almost every step of the way along a loop that is only 2 miles long. This could very well be the best short trail Michigan has to offer.

It is certainly one of the most spectacular spots in our state. In its final mile before emptying into Lake Superior, the Presque Isle descends more than 100 feet and in doing so has carved a rugged and steep-sided gorge and filled it with waterfalls.

Beginning in the park's Presque Isle Day-use Area, you waste no time in getting to the river. The trail immediately turns into a long stairway that leads you down to the Presque Isle and across the rushing water on an impressive swing bridge. From the middle of the bridge, it is an incredible view up stream. Presque Isle is by far the largest river to flow through the Porkies and its current is so strong that the whirlpool swirl of the water has carved perfect half-circles in the bedrock below you.

What appears on maps as a peninsula on the other side of the bridge is actually an island in the mouth of the river with a dry channel on one side that becomes flooded during high water. Trails cross the island to Lake Superior.

The marked route leads you to the dry channel on the east side, an intriguing spot. Crossing the channel you climb across layers of shale with a small waterfall in the background before reaching the other side of the gorge. Here the East River Trail begins with a steep climb out, topping off at the posted junction with the 16-mile long Lake Superior Trail. The East Trail heads south, climbing along the edge of the gorge and over masses of roots from the towering stand of virgin hemlock, white pine, and cedar. The trees are impressive here, but the walk can be challenging at times.

Backpackers climb out of the Presque Isle River Gorge along the West River Trail for the start of the Lake Superior Trail.

Eventually the trail descends to a bench overlooking Manabezho and Manido falls, a pair of thundering cascades just down river from each other. The first is Manabezho Falls, the most impressive cascade along the river. The falls make a 20 to 25-foot thundering drop over a rock ledge and create a heavy mist and a blanket of form. Another 100 yards upstream is Manido Falls, which descend 25 feet over a gradually declining set of rock ledges.

The trail stays on the edge of the gorge, and you can view a series of cascades for the next half mile until you arrive at Nawadaha Falls where the river tumbles 15 feet over a series of rock steps. At this point the trail swings away from the river until you break out at the South Boundary Road. Just on the other side of the bridge, you quickly leave the pavement and return to a needle-carpeted path to the West River Trail which leads through an impressive stand of hemlock.

The west side is a much easier hike. You stay near the river and for a half mile weave through the trees, passing Nawadaha Falls a second time. Eventually the trail dips down to the water itself for an unusual angle of the river. Looking downstream all you see is a flat placid surface of the Presque Isle. Hidden from view is Manido Falls. Imagine Indians paddling this stretch for the first time to be suddenly confronted with the 25-foot cascade.

Planking leads up the side of the gorge to the trail's impressive boardwalk section where large viewing areas put you right above Manido Falls and then Manabezho. You are so close you can feel their cooling mist on a hot afternoon. It is so impressive, you're disappointed when you soon return to the stairway that leads back to the day-use area.

The Ehlco Mountain Bike Complex is in the Ottawa National Forest but begins in the Porcupine Mountains and includes a number of unbridged stream crossings.

Chapter Ten

MOUNTAIN BIKING

Porcupine Mountains Wilderness State Park and the adjacent Ehlco Mountain Bike Complex offer a rare wilderness setting to mountain bikers along with some of the most challenging and technical riding in the western Upper Peninsula. Knobby-tire bikes are banned from the state park's 90-mile hiking trail system, but during the summer and fall they are permitted on most of the cross-country ski trails, a 15-mile system at the east end of the park.

The rugged ridges that are the Porkies make for adventure riding that demands you be prepared. Steep, rocky, uphills, and down hills are common, as are numerous water runoff crossings in early and late summer. If it has just rained, the moss-covered rocks and tree roots are slick, forcing you into a hike-and-bike adventure. The trails and intersections can be poorly marked at times, so it is best to get a map from the Wilderness Visitor Center before heading out.

Also keep in mind that this far north, the mountain biking season often doesn't get under way until late May or early June, and even then conditions will be sloppy. The best time to ride these trails is July through August. There are numerous trailheads to the cross country trail system, but the best place to park in the summer is at the Chalet in the Alpine Ski Area, just west of the Union Bay Campground. Pack along plenty of water and high-energy snacks before hitting the trails, and once on them figure on doubling your normal riding time.

Deer Yard and Superior Loop

Map on pages 136 - 137
Distance: 3 miles
Trail: Wide pathway
Direction: Counter clockwise
Deer Yard and Superior Loops can be combined for a 3-mile

ride that will be gentle on the mind and easy on the cardiovascular system. This ride begins with the Superior Trail across M-107 from the ski lodge, and takes you toward Lake Superior through a stand of impressive birch. If it has rained recently, there will be a number of puddle crossings because of the low-lying clay soil. A right at the first intersection takes you to the shores of Lake Superior and to White Birch Cabin, a warming shelter in the winter but a rental cabin the rest of the year. A right at the next intersection puts you on Deer Yard Trail to cap the first mile of the ride.

Deer Yard Trail is a bit more hilly and begins as a cobblestone pathway. Pass up the spur to Whitetail Cabin to cross a smallish stream and then venture through a towering stand of hemlocks—impressive trees to say the least.

Two miles into the ride you're hit with a sustained climb to M-107. Cross the paved road and continue the climb until topping out at an intersection. Head left and it's a long downhill run to the ski lodge.

West Vista Loop

Map on page 106
Distance: 13 miles
Trail: Wide pathway
Direction: Clockwise

This 13-mile ride is the park's grand loop for mountain bikers, a combination of several trails that lead you past three cabins, a yurt, and the spectacular views from both West Vista and East Vista. Pack a lunch and plenty of fluids. For most bikers this is a two to four-hour adventure. Or reserve the yurt or one of the cabins in advance (See chapter 3) and spend the night.

Again, the best place to begin is at the Alpine Ski Area Chalet. At the eastern end of the parking area is the start of the Nonesuch Trail, whose trailhead is marked with a mountain bike sign. The former tram road heads southeast and includes some knee-bending climbs before you reach a junction with River Trail 1.2 miles from the Chalet. Head east (left), passing a handful of interpretive signs and arriving at South Boundary Road in 1.6 miles. Continue with

River Trail on the east side of South Boundary Road as it skirts the Union River and crosses a few wet areas.

At 3.3 miles River Trail returns to South Boundary Road. Across the road is a trailhead and parking area for Union Spring Trail that the bike route continues on. After passing a posted spur to Union River Cabin, you cross Union River on a wide bridge and within 1.2 miles from South Boundary Road arrive at the intersection with River Trail. Continue with Union Spring Trail until it reaches an intersection where it swings south of the old Impoundment, 1.5 miles from South Boundary Road. At this point the trail is closed to mountain bikes and you need to head northwest (right) along the wide ski trail.

In the next 1.2 miles you'll pass a junction with Log Camp Trail, the small Crosscut Cabin that is available for rent and then arrive at the south end of Double Trail. Mountain bikes are prohibited from going any farther on what is labeled as Big Hemlock Trail on most maps. Turn north on Double Trail and be prepared for a gut-wrenching climb of almost 300 feet in elevation in a little more than a half mile. When you finally top out at 1,400 feet, turn left and follow the ski/bike trail for 0.6 mile past the West Vista Yurt to the outstanding views at the West Vista overlook, reached 7.2 miles into your ride.

Mountain bikes are prohibited from the Overlook Trail or the Government Peak that it leads to. To return to the Chalet, backtrack on the West Vista Ski/Bike Trail, past the junction to Double Trail and continue by coasting downhill to Triple Trail. Continue your downhill ride on Triple Trail for a half mile and then make a sharp left on Log Camp Trail, a junction reached 1.8 miles from the West Vista overlook.

In the next mile Log Camp Trail will lead you past Log Camp Cabin and then to the spur to East Vista, a fine viewing point where you can see miles of Lake Superior shoreline in the summer. In another 0.7 mile, Log Cabin Trail reaches a junction with River Trail. Turn east (left) here and in a mile turn north (left) on Nonesuch Trail to return to the Chalet parking area and end a 13-mile ride through northeast corner of the park.

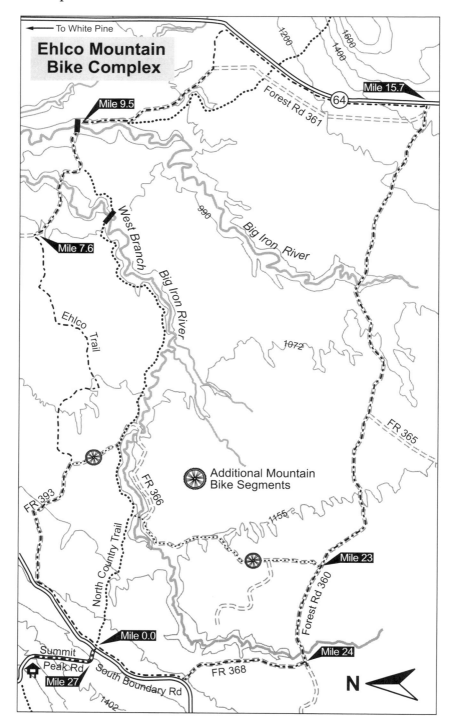

Ehlco Mountain
Bike Complex

To White Pine

Mile 9.5

Mile 7.6

West Branch

Big Iron River

Big Iron River

Ehlco Trail

Forest Rd 361

Mile 15.7

990

1200

1600

1400

1072

FR 365

Additional Mountain
Bike Segments

FR 393

FR 366

North Country Trail

1155

Mile 23

Mile 0.0

Summit
Peak Rd

Mile 27

South Boundary Rd

FR 368

Forest Rd 360

Mile 24

1402

N

Ehlco Mountain Bike Complex

Distance: 27 miles
Trail: Gravel roads and two-track
Direction: Clockwise

The Ehlco Mountain Bike Complex is a high adventure ride along overgrown logging roads and poorly-marked trails for people experienced in wilderness travel. The trails have not been maintained in years, and you must arrive with a compass, the proper topo maps, and emergency gear. The terrain is generally flat, but the trip is an extremely challenging one due to numerous beaver dams constantly flooding out the route and unbridged creeks and streams that must be forded.

The trailhead is on the south side of Porcupine Mountain Wilderness State Park, but the vast majority of the system lies in adjacent Ottawa National Forest. Most of the trail is old logging two-tracks that are 4- to 14-feet wide, but don't underestimate this ride due to the lack of technical single track. You will not see anybody else out there, and riders have been known to get turned around. Pack along water, parka, and some high-energy food (i.e. candy) just in case you have to spend more time in the woods than planned. Or even the night.

This route follows the perimeter of the system and includes fording the West Branch of the Big Iron River just before its confluence with the main stream. There is no bridge at this crossing and in the spring or after a particularly hard rain, the stream may be difficult if not impossible to cross. Forest roads are listed on maps but not along the trails. It's wise to check for conditions prior to embarking on your ride by contacting the Ontonagon Ranger District (906-884-2085, 1209 Rockland Road, Ontonagon, MI 49953).

From Summit Peak Road head left (northeast) on South Boundary Road to begin the trip in the Porcupine Mountains Wilderness State Park. Just past Mile 1, veer right onto a gravel logging road that is gated closed and unmarked. Within a half mile, the first of many beaver ponds will be encountered. These are adjacent to the trail but don't be surprised if they have flooded the route. At Mile 3 head left (east) at a junction onto a rough, dirt logging road. For almost the next 4 miles you'll follow this overgrown two-track through the most remote section of the tract, a forest of northern hardwoods, aspen, and white pine. This is perhaps the most challenging section in trying to stay on course.

You should arrive at Forest Road 361 within 7.7 miles from the start. Turn south (right) and in less than a mile you will arrive at the West Branch of the Big Iron River for the first time. You must ford the stream as there is no bridge and should do it cautiously during periods of high water. Once across, the most challenging segment of the route is behind you.

Forest Road 361 reaches the main branch of the Big Iron River at Mile 9.5. Thanks to the North Country National Scenic Trail, a bridge has been built across the river. On the other side is the access road that was used to build the bridge and now makes for easy riding for the next 2 miles. Eventually the posted route leaves FR 361 and follows a half mile of rough trail to reach paved M-64 at Mile 12.3.

Turn right on the state highway and follow the paved shoulder south for 3.4 miles to the junction of FR-360, reached at Mile 15.7. This forest road heads west as an open, gravel logging road. Near Mile 23 is the junction with FR 366, a cutoff spur that reaches FR 393 in 5 miles. The perimeter route continues west on FR 360, reaching the West Branch of the Big Iron River for the second time at Mile 24. The stream is considerably smaller here and can be crossed any time during the biking season. Turn right (north) on FR 368 and be prepared to get your feet wet crossing up to a half dozen ponds in the next mile or so. FR 368 returns you to South Boundary Road at Mile 25.7. The final leg of the ride is following paved South Boundary Road east for 1.2 miles to Summit Peak Road.

Hiking the North Country Trail

Unlike the Ehlco Mountain Bike Complex where the trails are not maintained, poorly marked, and hard to follow, the North Country Trail is just the opposite. The NCT splits the mountain bike tract in half and is well-cleared and easy to follow, thanks to the Peter Wolf Chapter (*www.northcountrytrail.org/pwf*) which built the 13-mile segment and is in charge of maintaining it.

The NCT is not open to mountain biking here but would make a great destination for an overnight backpacking trip. You can pick up the NCT where it crosses South Boundary Road near Summit Peak Road where there are trail signs. Parking and a registration station is located just up Summit Peak Road.

From here the NCT heads east along a somewhat level route through older growth hardwoods and hemlocks, following the bluffs above the West Branch of Big Iron River. Within a mile you leave Porcupine Mountains Wilderness State Park and enter the Ottawa National Forest and 7.6 miles from South Boundary Road you reach a bridge across the West Branch where there are some great spots to pitch a tent.

The next day would be a 5.4-mile trek to a trailhead area along M-64. Within 1.8 miles the NCT reaches a suspension bridge across Big Iron River that is shared with mountain bikers on the Ehlco trails. From there the trail heads south and climbs a ridge that gives way to views of the Porcupine Mountains before swinging more easterly to reach the state highway 3.6 miles from the Big Iron River bridge. There are plenty of camping possibilities at Big Iron River and Hooded Creek.

Chapter Eleven

WINTER IN THE PORKIES

To see that the Porcupine Mountains is not Boyne Highlands, Crystal Mountain, or any of Michigan's other glitzy ski resorts, all you have do is look inside the chalet.

Crockpots plugged in along the wall are slowly cooking lunch while the families are skiing outside. In the middle, there are a dozen people sitting around the open fireplace roasting hotdogs on sticks, and in the corner somebody's four-year-old just climbed into her sleeping bag for a mid-afternoon nap.

Better yet, take a look from the top. From the Eastern Summit you see the frozen Upper Peninsula shoreline all the way to Ontonagon, 20 miles away. From the Western Summit it is nothing but the endless blue of Lake Superior. The lake is so close there is a sensation when skiing that you will hit water before you hit the bottom.

No matter where you look, it is pretty obvious; downhill skiing in the Porkies is unique—so is cross-country skiing, snowshoeing, or just spending a night in a rustic cabin or yurt... a quarter mile from your car.

If you like the Porkies in the summer and are charmed by the mountains during autumn colors, you will be intrigued with the park during the winter when the snow is so deep it is chest high the minute your step out of your snowshoes. There is a different beauty to the land during February when Lake Superior's shoreline is a gallery of ice sculptures and the boughs of each pine are struggling under a layer of snow.

There is also a different crowd at the park—a very small one. You still have to reserve a cabin in advance, but lines at the chair lifts are as rare as spring weather in March, and cross-country skiing is a solitary pursuit into the woods.

*Snowshoer with backcountry skis enters the Porkies
for an overnight winter adventure.*

What's Available

Traditionally, winter arrives at the Porkies in mid-December and lasts to the first of April. At this time of the year the staff concentrates its activities and services to what is referred to as the Porcupine Mountains Winter Recreation Area in the northeast corner of the park. Access is strictly along M-107 from Silver City as South Boundary Road becomes part of a snowmobile route. The park road is not plowed beyond the entrance to the alpine ski area, which makes the Lake of the Clouds Escarpment the most scenic snowmobile destination in the state.

The Visitor Center is closed during the winter, and all backcountry permits and cabins rentals should be arranged at the park headquarters. One mile west of the Union Bay Campground is the alpine ski area with the downhill slopes, chalet, ski rental, and a large, two-tier parking lot. The parking lot is also used by cross-country skiers as nearby are the trailheads for the Nonesuch, Big Hemlock, and the Deer Yard Trail.

Along with downhill slopes and 42 kilometers of groomed Nordic tracks, three rustic cabins and four yurts are available for use during the winter. None of the other cabins or the campgrounds are open from December through April.

Alpine Skiing

The Porkies have a lot of things which no other downhill ski area can boast. For starters, it is surrounded by 60,000 acres of designated wilderness and few resorts in Michigan have the Porkies' powder. Warm air passing over frigid Lake Superior picks up moisture and deposits it as powder snow, up to 20 feet in a season. Winter temperatures are often 10 to 20 degrees warmer than inland ski areas.

The Porkies have a vertical drop of 787 feet which is one of the highest in the Midwest. The 14 original ski slopes lie within a 320-acre alpine area and are served primarily by a handle tow on the Bunny Slope and a triple chair lift to the Eastern Summit, a ride of 2,800 feet. Four runs; Ojibway, Cuyahoga, Agate, and the Porcupine Plunge are rated for advance/expert skiers with Agate Run and Cuyahoga departing from the Eastern Summit and extending the length of the mountain.

There are also seven intermediate runs, including Superior View which lives up to its name with spectacular views of the lake's frozen shoreline much of the way. Another intermediate slope, Ridge Run, is so scenic there is an observation deck with benches where skiers stop on a clear day to enjoy the view of the forested shoreline to Silver City.

The forests and that abundance of powder also makes the Porkies a paradise for backcountry downhill skiing. West of the original slopes is Everest, where 17 runs span a half mile wide glade. All rated double black diamond and are serviced by the Everest Express, a Snowcat tractor that transports skiers to the top. Other glade areas for backcountry enthusiasts have been developed between the original slopes, allowing the Porkies to boast of 42 runs with the longest exceeding a mile in length.

At the base is the chalet, a large A-frame lodge with three fireplaces, food service, lockers, modern restrooms, and a glass wall in the main lounge that overlooks the Hiawatha Run. Inside is a rental service for both downhill and Nordic equipment, a ski shop, and National Ski Patrol first aid services.

The downhill ski area is operated by Mount Bohemia (906-289-4105; *www.skitheporkies.com*) and is open Saturday, Sunday from 9:30 a.m. to 5:00 p.m. (EST) and Friday and Monday from 10:30 a.m. to 4:30 p.m. (EST).

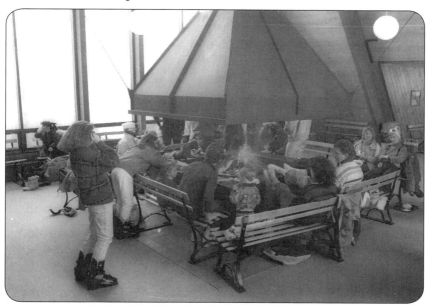

Skiers warm up around the chalet fireplace during the winter.

Cross-Country skiers follow the Big Hemlock Trail.

Cross-Country Skiing

Throughout the winter, the state park grooms and maintains 42-kilometers of Nordic ski trails or basically a 26-mile network of four main loops. The tracks are double set, posted with locator maps at major junctions and rated from "Easiest" and "More Difficult" to "Most Difficult."

The most practical place to start any cross-country trip is the chalet where nearby are three trailheads providing access to the Nonesuch Trail to the east, Big Hemlock Trail to the west, or Deer Yard that heads south of M-107 to the shores of Lake Superior. For the quickest access to the heart of the trail system or to enjoy the spectacular panoramas at East and West Vistas, cross-country skiers can purchase a one-trip tow ticket. The ticket can be used on the triple chair to reach the Eastern Summit from which several trails then quickly descend the back side of the mountain. Keep in mind however that loading and unloading the chair on skinny skis is more challenging than downhill skis.

The easiest trail is Superior Loop which can be handled by most beginners and includes a view of the ice formations along Lake Superior. The most challenging route is Big Hemlock, River, and Union Spring Trails, a 12-mile, 19-kilometer loop that is an all-day ski for most skiers.

TeleFest Ski Festival

What began in 1990 as an informal day of telemark skiing in the Porcupine Mountains has become TeleFest Ski Festival, a three-day celebration of backcountry skiing in early Feburary. Telemark skiing is a hybrid of downhill and cross-country skiing that is ideally suited to steep slopes, deep powder and backcountry adventures, which is why it found a home in the Porcupine Mountains. Telemark skis are wider with metal edges, but unlike downhill equipment the boot heel still remains free.

The heart and soul of the Telefest is the opportunity to try telemark demo equipment and sign up for an on-the-slope clinic to learn the telemark turn. Other activities include organized races on the downhill slopes, women's only clinics, backcountry tours and vendors displaying the latest ski equipment. Saturday ends with the Telefest Chili Cook-Off in the chalet followed by dancing late into the evening. Is there anything better after a full day of skiing and playing in the snow then a bowl of somebody's extra-spicy homemade chili?

The event is staged by Downwind Sports which has shops in Marquette and Houghton. For the exact dates and times of the Telefest or to register for clinics or events contact Downwind Sports or check its web site.

906-226-7112; 906-482-2500
www.downwindsports.com

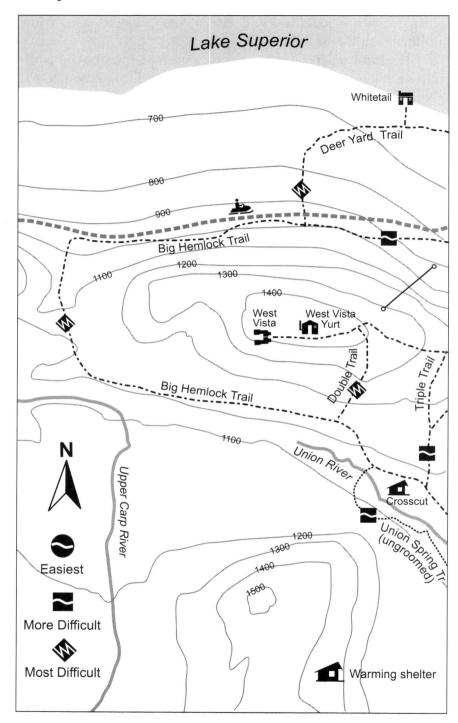

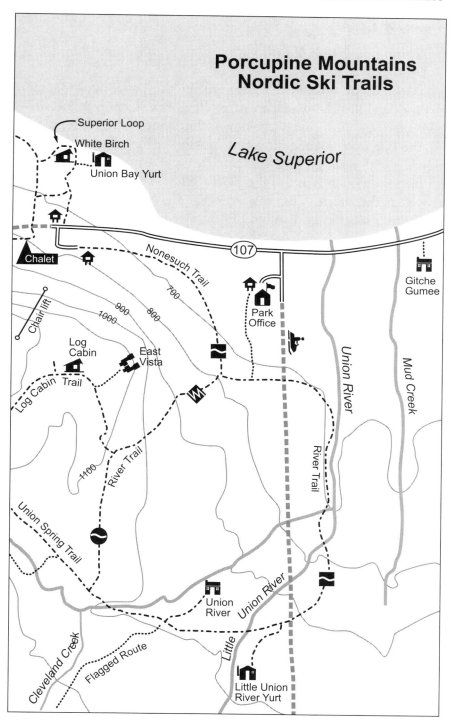

Porcupine Mountains Nordic Ski Trails

Lake Superior

Superior Loop

White Birch

Union Bay Yurt

Chalet

Nonesuch Trail

107

Gitche Gumee

Park Office

Chair lift

1000

900

800

700

Log Cabin

East Vista

Log Cabin Trail

River Trail

1100

Union River

River Trail

Mud Creek

Union Spring Trail

Union River

Union River

Cleveland Creek

Flagged Route

Little Union River

Little Union River Yurt

Superior Loop

Distance: 1.2 miles/2 km
Rating: Easiest

Most of the groomed routes within the park involve some steep downhill runs which to many beginner skiers translates to take-off-your-skies-and-walk-down the slopes. These are, after all, the Porcupine Mountains. But, luckily for families with young skiers, not all trails are that difficult.

Superior Loop is one of the most scenic ski trails in the Porkies as well as the shortest and easiest to handle. Maybe that's why its trailhead is located next to the Bunny Slope.

You no more than depart the tow rope area and enter the woods when you emerge at M-107 and are forced to high step it across the pavement. On the other side you enter a hardwood forest thick with paper birch that is especially enchanting on a cloudless day and continue on a gentle downhill run towards Lake Superior. You pass two posted junctions with the second one heading west along the Deer Yard Trail then emerge at the edge of the forest for a view of Lake Superior.

What a view! The lake is open and a deeper shade of blue than the sky, but the shoreline is usually piled high with ice and blanketed in white by the last snowfall. It is pretty evident from the tracks in the snow that most skiers cannot resist departing the trail and striding across the ice for a better view of the huge bergs, ice caves, and frozen arches that are formed during the long Upper Peninsula winter. *BUT BE CAREFUL TO AVOID SLIPPING IN!* Nearby is the White Birch Warming Shelter, ideal for a rest and a snack.

From the lakeshore you circle back and encounter your only steep slope on the run, but it's short and any mishap is done with the knowledge that you will soon be back at the chalet, kicking off your boots and roasting marshmallows at the open fireplace with a dozen other children and parents.

Cross-country skier on the Lake Superior Trail,
looking at Lake Superior.

Deer Yard Trail

Distance: 2.4 miles/4 km
Rating: Most Difficult

Deer Yard is a 4-km loop that is rated "Most Difficult" primarily because of a wicked downhill run toward Lake Superior at its west end. Thrill seekers will want to ski Deer Yard in a clockwise direction beginning at the Bunny Slope Trailhead. More cautious skiers will take a counter clockwise direction, beginning with the segment that the trail shares with the Superior Loop. At the second posted junction you head west, pass through an open marsh area, and then quickly arrive at the signposted spur to Whitetail Cabin, an eight-bunk unit overlooking Lake Superior.

Deer Yard continues west through a young forest of predominantly paper birch. It then enters a growth of stately hemlock and swings south to begin its steep climb to M-107. If you are coming in the other direction, this is a twisting, turning, rapid descent where you fly past huge pine trees. If you are climbing this section, take heart. At least you have more time to admire the timber.

Eventually you emerge at M-107, cross it, and pick up the trail on the other side. The final leg back to the chalet parallels the park road from above, gently descending most of the way until you are again mingling with the kid skiers back at the bunny slope.

Nonesuch & River Trails

Distance: 7.5 miles/12.5 km
Rating: More difficult

This is a scenic run, a 7.5-mile (12.5 kilometer) loop that can be handled by most intermediate skiers without too much difficultly. You can also turn this trip into an overnight adventure by reserving either the Union River Cabin or the Little Union River Yurt, both conveniently located roughly halfway.

In the southeast corner of the ski area parking is a trailhead with a posted map, displaying the start of the Nonesuch Trail. Adventurous skiers could also purchase a one-trip lift ticket and take the triple chair lift for a quick ski to East Vista and then follow Log Camp Trail to River Trail. This route is slightly shorter – 6.6 miles or 11 kilometers – and a bit easier as it avoids the hilly terrain at the beginning.

Nonesuch Trail does involve quite a bit of climbing in the first half mile. You no more than enter the forest when you are faced with a hill. The slope is steep; it is long and at the base it could also be wet in late winter. Signs will warn skiers coming from the other direction of both the steepness and the possibility of a wet trail.

Several more ascents are made and then you are rewarded with a long downhill run and from there it is a couple of strides to a posted junction with River Trail, reached in 1.2 miles. To the east (left) River Trail heads for South Boundary Road, a snowmobile route in the winter. To the south (right) it provides the quickest route to Union River Cabin. The trail is a relatively level run through a hardwood forest where within a mile you arrive at the posted junction with Log Camp Trail from East Vista. You remain on the level run and within another mile arrive at a posted junction.

To the west (right) is Union Spring Trail. The River Trail continues east (left) where you quickly descend a hill, cross gurgling Union River, and then climb to the posted junction to the Union River Cabin. From the cabin spur it is 0.6 mile until you reach a junction with the groomed trail to the Little Union River Yurt. The tent-like structure is a half mile to south, overlooking the small river and is another overnight option along this loop.

Just beyond the junction to Little Union River Yurt is the posted parking lot for hikers and South Boundary Road. On the other side of the snowmobile trail, the trail is posted with a map and a "More Difficult" diamond, but in this direction it is not a hard ski as you begin with a gentle downhill run through a forest that is a pleasant mix of leafless hardwoods and older pines. There is a pair of steep slopes and from the second one you descend to cross Union River again on a vehicle bridge that is used in the summer by campers.

A backcountry skier skis South Boundary Road
in April after the snowmobile season.

Once across the bridge you immediately re-enter the woods and begin the most beautiful stretch of the trail. For the next 20 to 30 minutes you ski between the Union River and towering wooded bluff on the other side. Here you'll usually find the snow deep and the creek open even during the coldest winters. This wooded area is often a quiet sanctuary from the winds off Lake Superior. Eventually the pines give way to a stand of all hardwoods, and you quickly emerge at South Boundary Road for the second time. Look both ways before crossing, snowmobilers seem to come out of nowhere.

On the other side, River Trail merges into a portion of the nature trail from the Visitor's Center, the reason for the interpretive signs. You eventually cross Jamison Creek and then come to the posted junction with Nonesuch Trail that you first passed from the parking lot. Head north (right) to return to the chalet, only this time most of the skiing will be downhill.

Big Hemlock & Union Spring Trails

Distance: 9 miles/15 km
Rating: Most Difficult

These two trails form the longest groomed loop in the park, a 9-mile (15 kilometer) ski into the backcountry of the Porkies. This is a day-long adventure for most skiers, and if the weather is nice many plan an extended break or even cook a meal at Crosscut Warming Shelter. If you want to shorten the loop to approximately a 6-mile ski, purchase a single ride lift ticket and descend the backside of the mountain from the Triple Trail. But be forewarned, it's a steep run. Eeeehaa!!!

Beginning at the trailhead in the southeast corner of the chalet parking lot, the first 3 miles of the loop is the same route with Nonesuch and River Trails that is described above. At the third posted junction head west (right) to continue on Union Spring Trail, a wide, double track trail. Within 0.6 mile you arrive at a junction with the ungroomed portion of Union Spring Trail that heads southwest (left) to the spring itself. The groomed Union Spring Trail bypasses the springs, but in the next mile passes the junction with Log Camp Trail and then arrives at Crosscut Warming Shelter. The small shelter is 4 miles from the chalet and is a great place to stroke up the wood stove and make a pot of hot chocolate or lunch.

Just beyond it to the west is the junction with the return of the ungroomed Union Spring Trail. From this direction the springs are a 0.8-mile side trip (1.6 miles roundtrip) that begins by crossing a scenic meadow ringed by trees just south of the junction. Once beyond the meadow you'll find the ungroomed Union Spring Trail is a narrow and winding trail through the thick woods or low-lying areas that are hopefully frozen, but the spring is worth the extra effort. Its observation deck may be heaped with snow, but most of the spring stays open during the winter, and you can still lean over the railing to view the bubbling sand at the bottom. There is a bench nearby and the area makes for a quiet and scenic spot to kick off the skis.

West from the junction groomed Union Spring Trail continues with a long half-mile climb. You top off at the posted junction with Double Trail spur from the West Vista and continue west on Big Hemlock Trail with a spirited downhill run. Another long climb follows, topping off in a stand of towering pines, many of them virgin hemlock.

Big Hemlock Trail remains in the pines for another stretch of scenic skiing until you reach its junction with Government Peak Trail, where the south end of Overlook Trail is posted with mileage for hikers. Head north (right) and in less than a mile you will climb through the hardwoods and pass the northern end of Overlook Trail. Just beyond the junction with the Escarpment Trail there's a wicked run downhill. Be careful as you could end up flying onto M-107, which at this time of year becomes a popular snowmobiler's route to the Lake of the Clouds.

The final 2.5 miles begins by following M-107 but twice dips into the woods to follow a trail above the road. Eventually you pass the posted junction to the Deer Yard Trail and then begin a gentle downhill run to the Chalet, ending up at the beginner's slope.

East Vista

Distance: 4.5 miles/7.5 km
Rating: Most Difficult

What could easily be the best panoramas in Michigan seen from cross-country skis are the East and West Vistas at the top of the park's alpine area, especially the West Vista. If the downhill area is open, both can be interesting trips up if you first purchase a single ride lift ticket at the chalet. Though more challenging to load and unload than for downhillers, cross-country skiers still utilize the triple chair even if they're lugging a backpack.

To reach the East Vista, head right from the triple chair at the top toward the beginning of the Hidden Valley Run. A sign marks where the Triple Trail departs into the woods and a yellow caution sign tips you off what lies ahead. Triple Trail is an extremely steep run where many skiers end up doing little more than snow plowing and praying for a half mile.

Triple Trail ends at a junction with Log Camp Trail, where you head east (left) to follow the gently rolling crest of the ridge. Within 1.2 miles you pass Log Camp Warming Shelter, a great place for an extended break or a ridge-top meal. Just 0.3 mile beyond it is the posted junction to East Vista. The short spur quickly emerges from the trees to climb the top of an open knob. Here you gaze east to view the Lake Superior shoreline to Silver City and beyond on a clear day while to the southeast is the copper mine.

The easiest way to return to the chalet is to continue along the Log Camp Trail, which makes a milder descent along the backside of the alpine area. From the East Vista spur, you bottom out at a posted junction with the River Trail in 0.6 mile and from there can head north (left) to pick up Nonesuch Trail and loop back to the ski area parking lot. In reverse this is also the easiest route to reach East Vista on the days the alpine area is closed.

Cross-country skiers take a break at the East Vista.

West Vista

Distance: 6.3 miles/10.5 km
Rating: Most Difficult

With the park's double chairlift out of commission, reaching the West Vista is a bit more challenging. If the alpine area is open, you can begin on the triple chair and at the top head west (right) along top of the downhill area, following the slope labeled Timber Lane. Within 0.6 mile you pass the defunct double chair lift and come to the posted West Vista Trail near the start of the Hemlock downhill slope.

West Vista Trail quickly passes a posted junction with Double Trail. Continue west (right) as the trail begins a long and somewhat steep climb. Within a quarter mile you top out to continue along the rolling crest of the ridge and pass the posted spur to West Vista Yurt. If you can reserve it in advance, this is a unique place to spend a winter evening in the Porkies. The views are stunning and if the northern lights make an appearance that evening you are truly blessed.

Beyond the yurt, you continue another 0.3 mile through the trees until you break out in the opening that is the West Vista. You can see Lake Superior from here along with the Upper Carp River Valley and the entire Escarpment. The view is best during the winter when the trees are leafless and you can see a sprawling valley that appears to be enclosed by a pair of mountain ranges. There isn't another panorama like this one in all of Michigan and maybe the entire Midwest.

From the West Vista you can follow Double Trail down the backside of the mountain at the second posted junction, then ski the remaining 4.5 miles of the Big Hemlock Trail. Keep in mind this is by far the most challenging downhill portion of the park's ski trail network. An easier return is to retrace your steps back to the alpine area and follow the Timber Trail (downhill ski run) to the East Vista trailhead and return via Log Camp and River Trails (see above section). Of course, if you know how to telemark then you can always follow the downhill skiers to the chalet.

Lake of the Clouds

Distance: 6 miles/9.5 km one way
Rating: More difficult

Skiers also follow the unplowed portion of M-107 to the Lake of the Clouds overlook, a spot that is as enchanting in winter as it is in summer. The skiing is easy, but be aware that this is a popular side trip with snowmobilers. For the more adventurous, a return along the Escarpment Trail is challenging, but the views are well worth the extra energy spent breaking a trail.

Whitetail Cabin during the winter with its view of Lake Superior.

Cabins & Yurts

Three cabins and four yurts within the park have been specially built for winter use and are the only ones that can be reserved from December through March. They should be reserved well in advance as they are popular destinations for cross-country skiers.

Gitche Gumee Cabin:

This cabin is just off M-107 and a mere 20-yard walk from where you park the car. The eight-bunk cabin is handicapped accessible but does not adjoin the Nordic trail system.

Whitetail Cabin:

This eight-bunk is a mile ski from the chalet along the east half of the Deer Yard Trail, an easy run. The cabin sits on a low bluff overlooking Lake Superior, and the ice formations along its shoreline and provide access to the rest of the trail network.

Union River Cabin:

This unit is located halfway around the 6.3-mile River/ Nonesuch Loop from the chalet. By purchasing a one-ride tow ticket and taking the triple chair to the East Vista, you can include the scenic viewing point the first day and add a sense of adventure with a ride to the top of the downhill slopes. The cabin is set along the Union River, a stream that is usually open throughout the winter. Like Whitetail, the cabin is well positioned away from the groomed trail for a secluded setting.

Union Bay Yurt:

Located in the Union Bay Campground, this yurt is reached during the winter via the Deer Yard Trail off of M-107 just west of the alpine parking lot. Follow it for a 0.3 mile to the second junction with the Superior Loop where a Union Bay Yurt sign has been posted. Head east (right) on Superior Loop to quickly reach the posted spur to the yurt. This side trail is short but ungroomed. The total ski from M-107 is only a half mile.

West Vista Yurt:

This stunning yurt, perched above the park's alpine area, can be reached within a mile by utilizing the triple chair lift. If the alpine area is closed, the route to the yurt is much more difficult. Many skiers begin at the chalet and head west to pick up the Big Hemlock Trail just downhill from the loading area of the double chairlift. They follow the groomed ski trail to the backside of the mountain where in 4.5 miles they reach the posted junction with the Double Trail. This trail is a bit of a climb but within a half mile puts you on top of the alpine area at West Vista Trail where the yurt is just a short distance to the west.

Little Union River Yurt:

Along on the same loop as Union River Cabin and only 1.5 miles away is this yurt, the first one to be set up in the park. Follow River Trail in a clockwise direction and the yurt is reached in 4 miles from the chalet. The second day would be almost a 5-mile ski back to your vehicle. You can shorten the outing each day and avoid hilly Nonesuch Trail by parking at the designated overnight parking area at the Park Headquarters and following the ungroomed interpretive trail to the River Trail.

The Route to Lost Creek Yurt

Lost Creek Yurt is the destination of one of the park's most adventurous winter outings. During the summer the yurt is an easy half mile hike from South Boundary Road. In the winter it's a challenging one-way journey of 6.3 miles with more than half of it along a flagged route. Most people carry both snowshoes and skis and need six hours or more to reach the yurt from the park headquarters. Needless to say, a morning start is essential as the days are short with sunset in December occurring just after 5 pm EST. You also need to be equipped with map and compass or GPS unit and be experienced in cross-country travel in case you lose the flagged route.

From the overnight parking area at the park headquarters, you begin on the ungroomed Visitors Center Nature Trail, following it 0.6 mile to the River Trail. Following the groomed cross-country ski trail in the clockwise direction you will reach the posted flagged route in 2.5 miles or 0.6 mile west of the Union Spring Trailhead.

The route is marked by orange plastic flagging with reflective silver stripes and is occasionally packed down by a snowmobile. The majority of people continue to use their skis but a recent snowstorm will leave the route buried and in which case snowshoes is preferred. Breaking that much trail in Nordic skis, even backcountry skis, can slow your party down to a mile an hour or even less and could quickly drain everybody's stamina.

This route generally follows old logging roads, but a section of it travels through open forest and along the way climbs several steep hills as it gains 500 feet in elevation. Within 3.5 miles of River Trail the route arrives at Lost Creek Yurt on the east side of the stream. The yurt is only a half mile away from the South Boundary Road which is a snowmobile trail from December through March, but snowmobilers are banned from entering the park here.

The yurt sleeps four and sits in a stand of old growth hemlock and maple, making it a beautiful spot in the winter. It's equipped with a dining table, benches, kitchen supplies, a wood stove, and a vault toilet outside. Watch that seat, it can be cold first thing on a frigid February morning.

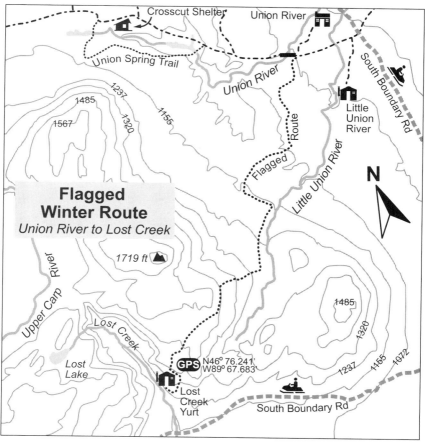

Appendix A
BACKPACKING ITINERARIES

The following are suggested backpacking itineraries with both daily and total mileage for various trips into the Porcupine Mountains Wilderness State Park. Each outing is a loop to eliminate the need for two vehicles. The treks are also arranged with short hikes the first day, the day most visitors arrive at the park, and follow the easiest direction of travel.

All backpackers must first register before entering the backcountry at either the Visitor Center or the park headquarters off of South Boundary Road. There is a nightly fee for backcountry camping and all camps must be a quarter mile from any cabin, scenic area such as rivers, or roads.

SIX-DAY OUTING	MILEAGE
Lake Superior Trailhead on M-107	0.0
1st Day: Lake Superior Trail to Lone Rock	4.9
2nd Day: Lake Superior Trail to Mouth of Little Carp River	5.9
3rd Day: Little Carp River Trail to Greenstone Falls Area	6.0
4th Day: Little Carp River Trail to Mirror Lake	5.8
5th Day: Government Peak Trail to Trap Falls Area	6.7
6th Day: Escarpment Trail to M-107 Trailhead	6.3
TOTAL	**35.6**

FIVE-DAY OUTING   MILEAGE

Lake Superior Trailhead on M-107	0.0
1st Day: Lake Superior Trail	
to Buckshot Landing	2.5
2nd Day: Lake Superior Trail	
to Mouth of Little Carp River	8.3
3rd Day: Little Carp River Trail	
to Greenstone Falls Area	6.0
4th Day: Little Carp River Trail	
to Mirror Lake	5.8
5th Day: North Mirror Lake Trail	
to M-107 Trailhead	4.3
TOTAL	**26.9**

FOUR-DAY OUTING   MILEAGE

Trailhead on Little Carp River Road	0.0
1st Day: Little Carp River Trail	
to Lily Pond	2.5
2nd Day: Correction Line Trail	
to Big Carp River	5.3
3rd Day: Big Carp River Trail	
to Mouth of Little Carp River	5.6
4th Day: Little Carp River Trail	
to Trailhead	7.0
TOTAL	**20.4**

FOUR-DAY OUTING   MILEAGE

Lake Superior Trailhead on M-107	0.0
1st Day: Lake Superior Trail	
to Buckshot Landing	2.5
2nd Day: Lake Superior Trail	
to Mouth of Big Carp River	7.0
3rd Day: Big Carp River Trail	
to Mirror Lake	7.1
4th Day: North Mirror Lake Trail	
to M-107 Trailhead	4.0
TOTAL	**20.9**

THREE-DAY OUTING	MILEAGE
Trailhead on Little Carp River Road	0.0
1st Day: Little Carp River Trail	
to Cross Trail Junction	1.0
2nd Day: Cross Trail	
to Mouth of Little Carp River	5.8
3rd Day: Little Carp River Trail	
to Trailhead	7.0
TOTAL	**13.8**

THREE-DAY OUTING	MILEAGE
South Mirror Lake Trailhead	0.0
1st Day: South Mirror Lake Trail	
to Mirror Lake	3.5
2nd Day: North Mirror Lake Trail	
to Big Carp River	9.1
3rd Day: Correction Line Trail	
to Summit Peak Road Trailhead	6.0
TOTAL	**18.6**

THREE-DAY OUTING	MILEAGE
Government Peak Trailhead on M-107	0.0
1st Day: Government Peak Trail	
to backcountry campsites	1.5
2nd Day: Government Peak Trail	
to Mirror Lake	6.7
3rd Day: North Mirror Lake Trail	
to M-107 Trailhead	3.8
TOTAL	**12.0**

THREE-DAY OUTING   MILEAGE

	MILEAGE
Lake Superior Trailhead on M-107	0.0
1st Day: Lake Superior Trail to Lone Rock	4.9
2nd Day: Lake Superior Trail to Shining Falls area	5.5
3rd Day: Big Carp River Trail to Lake of the Clouds Overlook	8.2
TOTAL	**18.6**

TWO-DAY OUTING   MILEAGE

	MILEAGE
South Mirror Lake Trailhead	0.0
1st Day: South Mirror Lake Trail to Mirror Lake	3.0
2nd Day: Little Carp River Trail to Trailhead via Lily Pond	5.3
TOTAL	**8.3**

TWO-DAY OUTING   MILEAGE

	MILEAGE
Government Peak Trailhead on M-107	0.0
1st Day: Overlook Trail to West Vista Yurt	1.9
2nd Day: Overlook Trail to M-107 Trailhead	2.1
TOTAL	**4.0**

Appendix B
QUICK REFERENCE

The following are the web addresses and phone numbers to a variety of organizations and agencies that can assist in planning any trip to Upper Peninsula:

Porcupine Mountains Wilderness State Park
www.michigan.gov/porkies
(906) 885-5275
Contact the park for information about backpacking, cabin rentals, campground reservations, or winter activities. Many of its brochures can be downloaded online.

Friends of the Porkies
www.porkies.org
This volunteer group can provide information about its many activities in the park including the Porcupine Mountains Music Festival and its Folk School.

Ottawa National Forest
www.fs.fed.us/r9/ottawa
(906) 932-1330
The Porkies are practically surrounded by the Ottawa National Forest, which offers a wide range of hiking and backpacking opportunities as well as many rustic campgrounds.

Porcupine Mountains Convention and Visitors Bureau
(906) 884-2047
www.porcupinemountains.com
The bureau can provide information on lodging and campgrounds just outside the Porkies and throughout Ontonagon County.

Upper Peninsula Travel & Recreation Association
www.uptravel.com
(906) 774-5480 or (800) 562-7134

For additional information on lodging, attractions, and campgrounds throughout the Upper Peninsula.

MichiganTrailMaps.com

www.michigantrailmaps.com

A web site with a wealth of information and trail maps for hiking and backpacking throughout the state.

The Michigan Department of Natural Resources

Parks & Recreation Division
www.michigan.gov/dnr
(517) 373-9900

For other information about other Michigan state parks including campground facilities and hiking opportunities.

A backpacker enjoying the view from an escarpment along the Big Carp River Trail.

INDEX

ABOUT THE AUTHOR

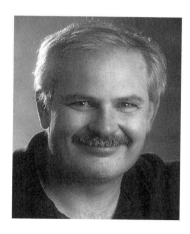

Jim DuFresne is an outdoor writer based in Clarkston, Michigan and author of more than a dozen wilderness/travel guidebooks. His books cover areas from Alaska and New Zealand to Michigan's own Isle Royale National Park. He also contributes recreational outdoor and travel articles to a variety of magazines and is a regular contributor to Michigan Blue Magazine.

DuFresne is a journalism graduate from Michigan State University and the former outdoors and sports editor of the Juneau Empire, where in 1980 he became the first Alaskan sportswriter to ever win a national award from Associated Press. Shortly after that, DuFresne spent a winter in New Zealand to backpack and write his frist book, *Tramping in New Zealand* (Lonely Planet Publications). Six editions and 25 years later, *Tramping in New Zealand* is the world's bestselling guidebook to backpacking in that country. *DuFresne's Isle Royale National Park: Foot Trails & Water Routes* (Mountaineer Books) has been in publication in various editions for more than 20 years.

Among DuFresne's other titles include *Michigan's Best Campgrounds* (Thunder Bay Press), *Twelve Classic Trout Streams: A Handbook for Fly Anglers* and *Backpacking in Michigan* (University of Michigan Press), *50 Hikes in Michigan* (Backcountry Publications), and *Road Trip: Lake Michigan*, *Hiking in Alaska*, and *Alaska* (Lonely Planet Publications).

Other books by

JIM DUFRESNE

Isle Royale National Park: Foot Trails & Water Routes

Backpacking in Michigan

50 Hikes in Michigan

Twelve Classic Trout Streams: A Handbook for Fly Anglers

Best Hikes for Children: Michigan

Michigan State Parks

Michigan: Off The Beaten Path

Michigan's Best Campgrounds

The Complete Guide to Michigan Sand Dunes

Road Trip: Lake Michigan

Tramping in New Zealand

Alaska

Hiking in Alaska

Wild Michigan